The Art of Practice:

Accelerate Your Learning, Quickly Build Expertise, and Perform Like a Pro

By Peter Hollins,

Author and Researcher at petehollins.com

Table of Contents

Part 1: You Need a Strategy

Maybe you looked at the title of this book and wondered, "How to practice? How to practice *what?*"

Therein lies the whole problem. When it comes to learning anything new—whether that's an instrument, a sport, a new academic subject, a language, or some new technical skill—many of us start with what seems like an obvious first step: the material itself.

We dive in, follow any pre-made curriculums set before us, and hope that whatever talent and intelligence we have is enough to see us through. In other words, we have absolutely zero strategy. In one word, this book is about just that: strategy. It's about **learning about learning** and making sure that when it comes to growth and development, we are not leaving things to chance, but consciously, deliberately creating an experience that will carry us from where we are to where we want to be.

If you picked up this book, chances are there is something you are currently trying to learn. Whatever it is, however, your path to mastery will tend to take some predictable twists and turns. That's because human beings tend to learn in predictable ways. Understand these ways, and you understand how to structure your efforts in learning.

The good news is that, ultimately, intelligence, talent, and even passion only take you so far. And you definitely don't need "ten thousand hours" either. **A solid plan of attack, the right mindset, and plenty of contingency planning will carry you a lot further than any raw aptitude.** And these are all things that you can learn.

The Deliberate Practice Roadmap

Let's meet Ellie, who wants to learn to paint better. She has loads of natural talent and has been arty all her life, but she works as an estate agent, and combined with parenting two kids, there's not a lot of time to devote to the painting dream. People have always praised her work, but if she's honest, Ellie is afraid that she doesn't have "what it takes." Sometimes, late at night she'll steal an hour or two to herself to sit with a sketchbook and some watercolors. This is pretty relaxing, but she's more or less doing the same thing she always does and knows deep down that this time isn't really making her a better artist.

One day she takes a leap and signs up with a local class and commits to a course that will force her to enter a professional portfolio for her final assessment. With a real goal on the horizon, she feels suddenly fired up to really push herself. She starts to realize she'll have to up the ante and get serious about all the skills she hasn't yet mastered, and exactly how she can work toward them step by step. The evenings spent doodling won't cut it anymore!

Soon, she hits a wall again, though. She's following her course curriculum and learning day by day, but she needs more help seeing around her blind spots—in other words, she needs a mentor. Another painter who is doing the kind of work she wants to do; someone who can work with her and give her guidance, support, and professional feedback she can really work with. Ellie finds a painting coach and, within a year, is astonished at how far she's come. Not only has she completed her course and submitted a portfolio, but her technique and range have gone further than she ever imagined, and she is soon in the process of organizing her first exhibit at a local gallery.

Looking back, she sees that the problem wasn't a lack of talent or passion for the craft. It wasn't even a lack of practice because, after all, Ellie had spent an hour or two every day for years on her painting. Rather, the problem was simply a poor approach and a lack of an organized, intentional method for learning.

Practice is important, but not all practice is created equal. There are **three different types of practice**: naive practice, purposeful practice, and deliberate practice, each representing varying levels of effectiveness in skill improvement.

1. **Naive Practice:** This is the most common type of practice where individuals go through the motions but without specific goals or challenges. They perform tasks in the same way repeatedly without pushing themselves to improve. This was Ellie in the evenings after the kids had gone to bed and she had some time to doodle and paint. This kind of practice does not typically lead to significant progress

beyond a certain acceptable level of performance. In Ellie's case, her innate talent had taken her to a particular level, and her daily practice was more or less maintaining her there.

2. **Purposeful Practice:** Purposeful practice is an improvement over naive practice. It involves setting specific and measurable goals, focusing intently on the task at hand, seeking feedback, and pushing oneself beyond one's comfort zone. This was Ellie realizing she needed to give herself a push and sign up for a challenge—the art course. Purposeful practice allows for small, incremental improvements that lead to more significant advancements over time. For hobbyists, this level may be sufficient. But you certainly don't have to stop here.

3. **Deliberate Practice:** Deliberate practice is the most effective form of practice, and it's primarily applied in well-established and competitive fields. It involves purposeful practice but adds two essential elements: a well-defined and rigorous field with clear distinctions between experts and novices, *and* a skilled coach who can provide tailored practice strategies and feedback. Deliberate practice is

informed and guided by the accomplishments of expert performers and has a clear roadmap for improvement. For Ellie, this meant getting a painting coach to work directly with her in a way she could never achieve on her own.

Deliberate practice is a highly effective method for rapid skill improvement. It entails intense and structured practice focusing on essential aspects of the skill being mastered. The goal is to extend one's capabilities and push beyond current limits. You'll see this kind of endeavor whenever you see professional athletes, musicians, performers, or creatives of all kinds aiming for the very highest levels of output. But deliberate practice is not just for celebrities and superstars—it can help you, too.

Deliberate practice is not really a *what*, but a *how*. It's like having a clear roadmap for your own development. Learning of this intensity happens outside your comfort zone—because that's the point. Expanding yourself beyond your current abilities takes a willingness to constantly stretch and challenge yourself to something bigger than your current reality.

It involves clear and specific goals aimed at improving particular aspects of performance. Complete focus and conscious actions are required, not just passive adherence to instructions, and certainly not just waiting for inspiration or doing what feels easy or comfortable.

Feedback is essential, with learners progressively learning to self-assess and adjust their efforts. Deliberate practice often involves refining previously acquired skills by honing specific aspects of those skills. Ultimately, it leads to transformation and significant personal growth through deep engagement in the training process.

Well, first things first: perhaps this roadmap metaphor needs a little further explanation. The "road" to mastery is not straight. It's more like one of those roads you find leading into airport parking lots—it spirals up and up, covering the same ground over and over again, but each time at a higher level. An important part of this process is your teacher (or something/someone who acts like a teacher) who can initiate you properly into that "virtuous cycle." This is what that looks like:

The Deliberate Practice Roadmap

1. **Find a Teacher or Substitute Teacher:** To engage in deliberate practice effectively, having a teacher or coach is essential. The right person can provide guidance, help you set specific goals, and offer useful feedback you can act on. If a direct coach is unavailable, that's no problem. Instead find an expert in your field to study and emulate. Use them to help you set small, concrete goals and establish your own feedback mechanism.

   Let's say you want to study piano: Seek guidance from a piano teacher who can assess your current level, provide tailored instruction, and set specific goals for improvement. If access to a teacher is limited, consider learning from online resources or studying the performances of skilled pianists to emulate their techniques. You can guess that a big part of getting this step right is making sure that the people you identify truly are masters, not just in their work, but with the teaching process itself. An experienced piano teacher, for example, may be a better bet than a distinguished concert pianist who doesn't know the first thing about teaching.

2. **Assess Your Limits:** Using the help of your teacher, identify the boundaries of your current skill level by recognizing your weaknesses or areas for improvement. If you can, do this without judgment or negativity—just get really neutral and factual about it. (We'll cover mindset in the next chapter.)

For example, evaluate your piano playing to identify areas that need improvement, such as finger dexterity, rhythm, sight-reading, or playing complex musical pieces. Ask your teacher to assess you and identify areas you most need to focus on right now. They may see something you don't— for example, the fact that a big obstacle is not your technique, but your confidence with performing.

3. **Set a Reaching SMART Goal:** Inspired by these identified limits, choose a specific skill to develop and set a goal *just beyond* your current capabilities, so you challenge yourself without feeling overwhelmed. For example, choose a specific aspect of piano playing that you want to enhance, like improving finger coordination or working on breathing so you're less nervous during a performance.

    Set a SMART goal (specific, measurable, achievable, realistic, and time-limited), but choose something that stretches your abilities while remaining achievable within a reasonable time frame. In other words, don't aim too small.

4. **Practice with Focus:** Armed with this insight, your practice can actually *mean* something. Engage in focused practice, giving your complete attention to the task you've identified. Pour all your energy and attention into it until you've achieved the goal.

    In our piano example, this might mean daily practice sessions where you focus intently on proper hand positioning, dynamics, and accuracy while playing. Or perhaps you gradually expose yourself to playing in front of others until you feel comfortable and confident doing so. Whatever it is, your practice is focused—you apply yourself to whatever brings you closer to your goal, and only on that.

5. **Get Feedback:** Use a feedback mechanism, ideally from a skilled teacher or coach, to assess your performance relative to your goals and to identify areas for improvement.

For example, you seek feedback from your piano teacher (or hey, if they're like the piano teachers I know, they'll let you know!). You could alternatively use recordings to self-evaluate your progress and pinpoint areas that require further attention. And then, because we're on a spiral road that never really ends, we feed straight back into the next step: identifying limits and gaps in knowledge or mastery. How well did you do? Let's say you achieved nine out of ten goals. Have a little celebration and then—you guessed it— get to work on making that final unachieved goal the sole focus of your practice from that point on.

That is, unless you get frustrated/overwhelmed/depressed/bored and decide to drive off the spiral road and put yourself out of your misery. That may be an exaggeration, but you get the point: **One of the biggest problems with learning is maintaining motivation**.

It's essential to push against the tendency to become complacent and lose the drive to progress. People often stop pushing themselves when they feel they are "good enough" (Nine out of ten? That's great, isn't it?) and opt for relaxation over further improvement.

To stay motivated, weakening reasons to quit and reinforcing reasons to continue is crucial. That's going to change with each loop on the road. Strategies for maintaining motivation include staying physically active and getting enough sleep, eliminating distractions, forming a habit around practice, setting time limits to avoid burnout, celebrating achievements, committing to overcoming plateaus, and forming a supportive group of like-minded individuals to provide mutual motivation. We'll explore these strategies and more in subsequent chapters.

Slow Practice

Slow practice is a fundamental technique used in learning and development—often in music. **The main principle involves playing passages of music at a slower tempo than intended and gradually increasing the speed with each repetition until the correct tempo is achieved.** This method helps in several aspects of musicianship, such as fingering, technique, articulation, and understanding the melodic and harmonic structure of the music.

The only snag is that most students tend to hate slow practice! It can get boring, and the tendency to want to rush and get to the end is strong. This usually comes down to focusing too much on the **outcome** (how awesome you're going to look shredding that violin) and not on the **process** of plodding slowly through a sequence again and again. The unavoidable fact is, however, that learning takes place in the process, not the outcome.

To use slow practice effectively, discipline is essential. The process requires commitment and patience. By consistently practicing at a slower pace, the piece becomes ingrained in both the fingers and the mind, leading to better performance.

American bassoonist William Short is someone who has embraced the slow practice as a valuable learning tool. He starts at a slow pace and gradually increases it in subsequent repetitions. While this is happening, he is focused mentally on precision and deep comprehension of the music. Every time he speeds up a tiny bit, he drills that sequence and cements it into his body and mind a little further.

You don't have to be a musician to benefit from this method, though. Take a look:

How to Apply Slow Practice

Step 1. Uh, go slowly

Whether it's a golf swing, your elevator pitch, a dance move, or an athletic maneuver, run through the task as a sequence, doing it very slowly to start. Your pace should allow you to remain relaxed and alert, and you should perform at the level you are able to maintain perfect form. You don't want to make even a teeny tiny mistake here. If you do, slow it down even further—the right speed is often way slower than you think. Repeat a few times.

Step 2. Try it full speed

Once you're comfortable doing it slowly, dial up the speed to the ordinary performance level. Do a natural golf swing, try that deadlift, or attempt a triple pirouette. Now, as a warning: this might go spectacularly well, and it might . . . not. It doesn't matter. Your goal is not to deliver perfection but just expose yourself to what the goal speed is. If it's a disaster, stop. There's no point doing it again and inadvertently training that disaster. If you do well, give it a few more attempts.

Step 3. Stop and assess

Finally, you want to actually evaluate what happened. Go beyond whether it worked or didn't, and ask exactly what worked and, more importantly, why did it work? What was a little weak? The point of narrowing in on these things is that you can then repeat the process, starting again with slow practice, but this time focus on that one little tricky bit (yup, we're on the spiral road again!). The next time you try it at full speed, it will be different. Ask how it's different, make adjustments, and repeat.

Understanding Energy Levels

Let's say that you have a passion for the bassoon so vast and all-consuming that it leaves your friends and family a little baffled. You have a picture of a good-looking bassoon hanging up in your room and a tiny pencil on your desk shaped like a bassoon. You are a devoted disciple and show up diligently to your bassoon lesson every day without fail, scarcely able to contain yourself.

To start off the two-hour lesson, you begin with a few scales (easy peasy) and some warmup exercises (you don't really need a warmup, though; your heart is just always on fire for the bassoon, obviously). But your teacher is a methodical person and wants you to work through the exercise book. So you do the exercises, and with ease. Then about an hour and twenty minutes into the lesson, you're ready to start with the good stuff: the Sonata in F Minor by Telemann.

The opening of the second movement is a thing of sublime beauty, you feel. You hear it in your dreams at night. It's a great piece, but it's also really, really difficult. You tackle it confidently, but by the time you get to the second movement, something awful happens: You get tired. You start out okay, but you soon fumble and quickly lose your pizzazz. A few sad goose noises later and it's all over. You're a little bit heartbroken.

Your methodical teacher says not to worry, practice makes perfect. He'll see you tomorrow again, and then you'll give it another try. But the next day when you sit down, he opens the exercise book once more and asks you to begin at the beginning, with the same old scales and warmup exercises . . .

You can see what's happening.

The person in our example has high motivation (uh, suspiciously high motivation) to play the bassoon. And yet, this doesn't help them avoid the natural fatigue that comes with practice and learning. **Energy isn't infinite. In fact our energy levels rise and fall in a predictable pattern, and if we wish to make the best use of that limited energy, we need to be strategic** (there's that word again!) and plan our activities accordingly.

In practice sessions, there are three types of energy to consider, and it's important to learn how to invest in each of them properly. **Your energy tends to be high at the start of a practice session, and steadily fall.** Your current maximum skill level tends to stay constant. Usually, traditional lessons and practice sessions start slow and build up so that your maximum skill level is reached only after quite some time has passed—i.e., after you're already getting tired.

People who excel at high-quality practice tend to practice new and difficult skills either at the beginning or middle of their session instead, avoiding the end where they might have lower energy. In other words, they reverse the conventional order and start with the most challenging thing *first*.

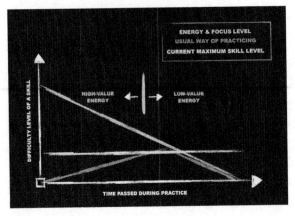

The above diagram basically shows us that there are two energy modes: high-value energy, which is focused and active, and low-value energy, which is passive and less productive. High-value energy is available at the beginning and stays until approximately the middle of the practice session. From that point on, low-value energy takes over, and it lacks the necessary focus and productivity for effective progress.

The current maximum skill level refers to the highest level of difficulty that a person can achieve in performing a skill at the present moment. It is unique to each individual and represents the edge of their abilities, where they are pushing themselves to their limit but are still capable of handling the challenge.

The **"new-level skill"** is given priority and takes up a significant portion of practice time, either during the "high-value" or "good-value" phase. The **"high-value"** phase serves as an intense warmup to prepare for practicing the new skill effectively.

Naturals rarely use the **"low-value"** phase, and they may stop practicing once they reach this level. However, this doesn't mean they neglect their routines entirely—it's still a great opportunity to practice things like scales. Naturals prioritize progress and constantly push their limits with harder skills, but they eventually do come back to perfect their routines.

Their approach makes it easier to transition from challenging skills to routines, as energy levels sync well. Of course, it's important not to overdo it or attempt skills *far* beyond current capabilities—that will just overwhelm and demoralize you. A general guideline is to work at first on skills that are about five to ten percent above the current maximum skill level. It's that magic place just a few steps outside your comfort zone.

If you are doing slow practice as described in the previous section, you might choose to lead every practice session with the single task that you are choosing to focus on. This may be a little confusing, because slow practice rests on the idea of *building up* to the big thing, while the approach described above encourages you to dive in and do the big thing first. So which is the right way?

Look closely and you'll see that *both* ways are.

So, you might identify the second movement of the sonata as your most important skill to master. This is your "big thing." You make sure you work on this first, when your energy levels are highest. However, the first ten minutes of your lesson may be slow practice again— slowly drilling through that second movement again and again, then doing it at normal speed, etc. It's essentially the opposite of waiting till late in the lesson to run at full speed through the most difficult task.

Here are some more tips to better manage your natural energy levels:

Reverse the Practice Order

Instead of starting with routine-based skills and gradually increasing difficulty, try reversing the order. Begin with the most challenging skill or technique, using your peak energy and focus at the start of the session. Progress to easier skills as your energy decreases. This way, you can dedicate your high-value energy to pushing your current maximum skill level, leading to more effective progress.

One way to structure this is to use the tail end of a practice session for consolidating what's already been learned earlier on. So, once you've already worked on your most challenging skill or technique, you can gradually move it to the later end of the session as you make room for new skills and techniques. Another great thing about this approach is that you'll be feeling more capable after tackling a challenge and can carry some of that confidence forward. If you have already felt that you can do the big thing, the smaller things that follow will seem even easier and more enjoyable. Do it the other way around, though, and you may just make yourself bored with the easy stuff and intimidated by the hard stuff.

Let's say you're practicing the violin (that bassoon obsession was a little unhealthy). At the start of your lesson, work on challenging pieces, difficult bowing techniques, or intricate fingerings—whatever it is you've identified as your chosen challenge. As your energy gradually decreases, transition to practicing scales or exercises that you have already mastered, using your remaining energy to refine and solidify those skills.

Embrace the Growth Mindset

Instead of fearing the loss of skills you have already achieved, adopt a growth mindset focused on continuous improvement and everything that you can still learn. Understand that progress requires pushing your boundaries and seeking new challenges. Prioritize improvement over maintaining existing skills, and trust that your routines will improve naturally as you progress. If many of us are honest, we sometimes get a little too comfortable with what we already know. We sit down for an hour to practice something new but only dedicate a tiny fraction of that hour to genuinely new material—the rest may be familiar tasks we run through just because it doesn't take much effort but still feels like we're accomplishing something.

With a growth mindset, you'll be more open to taking on new, demanding violin pieces and techniques, for example, which will lead to significant progress over time.

Be Aware of Cognitive Biases

Educate yourself about the cognitive biases that can impact decision-making and progress in practice. Recognizing and understanding these biases can help you make more rational and effective choices in your training. It's no exaggeration to say that certain unchallenged beliefs and assumptions about learning can be an enormous impediment to learning, canceling out all your effort and intention. The biggest threat is almost never lack of talent or intelligence; more likely it's another dangerous duo: fear and laziness (which we'll charitably call "comfort orientation").

Two big biases to watch out for when it comes to better practice are:

The **anchoring bias**, which might lead you to fixate on specific practice routines or techniques that you are used to, even if they are not yielding the desired progress. The human brain tends to overvalue the first piece of information it's exposed to and place more weight and importance on that. While we can certainly use that to our advantage, a downside of this mental shortcut is that we tend to fall into habits and just passively assume that the habit is the best or only way to do things.

In our violin example, you might keep returning to the same old practice books or list of exercises that you've stuck with for years just because of the momentum of habit. Your routines and habits *may* accidentally be just the right ones for you, but without consciously appraising their value, you won't really know. Getting too attached to any one technique or method may keep you quite limited so that you essentially end up *practicing how to be the same*—i.e., stagnation and plateauing are the only natural outcome.

Additionally, be cautious of the **status quo bias**, which could make you reluctant to explore new, more challenging pieces or techniques. Basically, if what you're doing sort of works, you feel that you might as well maintain the status quo, especially since trying something new may mean more effort and risk. Challenge yourself to break away from familiar routines and be open to trying new approaches and materials to reach higher skill levels.

A big caveat is due, however. Bearing in mind the importance of deliberate and strategic practice, it's worth paying attention to *what* you schedule to coincide with your highest energy level. You won't get very far if you don't already have a clear idea of your long- and medium-term goals, nor will you succeed if you're not really clear on what your strengths and weaknesses are (that's where your teacher comes in handy). Returning to our roadmap, we can only "practice with focus" if we have completed the previous step, i.e., "have SMART goals in place."

The Stages of Mastery

How do human beings learn to do anything new? Have you ever considered what that process is actually like? If you're like most people, it's something you've never paid much attention to—you may have just taken your ability to learn, develop, and acquire mastery for granted, perhaps only becoming aware of it when it didn't work as you thought it should.

But learning follows predictable and observable patterns. We can develop theories about what learning is and how it unfolds, and then use these theories to help us devise a way of learning that works *with* our innate nature, rather than vainly tries to push *against* it (which is not only exhausting and demoralizing, but also really inefficient).

The "stages of learning" is one such framework that helps individuals understand their progress in acquiring new skills. The four stages are briefly summarized like this:

1. Unconscious incompetence: you don't know how, and you don't know that you don't know
2. Conscious incompetence: you don't know how, but you know that you don't know

3. Conscious competence: you are beginning to know how, and you know it
4. Unconscious competence: you know how, but you're beyond being aware of it

Let's take a closer look.

Unconscious incompetence: At this stage, the person lacks awareness of what they need to know or learn to perform a specific skill effectively. They may not even realize that there is a skill they need to develop.

Conscious incompetence: In this phase, individuals become aware of the skills they lack and the areas they need to improve. They recognize their incompetence and may feel challenged by the complexity of the skill they are trying to acquire.

Conscious competence: At this stage, the person has acquired the skill but requires conscious effort and focus to demonstrate it successfully. They can perform the skill, but it still requires concentration and practice to execute it effectively.

Unconscious competence: This is the final stage of learning, where the individual has achieved mastery of the skill. Performing the skill becomes effortless and automatic, requiring no conscious effort or thought. They can combine skills or create unique blends effortlessly.

You might be wondering how it helps to know about these four stages. Practical implications of these stages include gaining awareness and self-confidence during the initial learning phase and continuing to practice and refine the skill even in the mastery stage to maintain proficiency and possibly combine it with other skills for even greater expertise. In other words, it's about pitching your efforts to match the level you're actually in. Depending on where you are, you will need to focus on different needs and acquire different skills.

Let's take a look at each stage in turn, with an example that will demonstrate just how much a person's needs and challenges shift as they improve in any chosen task. The task for our example is one that many of us have had to master: driving a car.

The first stage is unconscious incompetence—and ignorance is bliss, as they say. You don't know what you don't know, and you may completely lack comprehension about just how "bad" you are at the skill, or what it takes to acquire it. In our example, let's say you're a plucky teenager who has yet to earn their learner's permit, and glibly thinks, "Man, driving looks pretty easy. I bet I can get the hang of it in no time. What a waste of time to have to get this stupid learner's permit first . . ."

Therein lies one of the biggest risks at this level: overestimating your own abilities. (Isn't it funny how the people who know the least often think they know the most? That's not just teenagers, sadly, but most humans!) When you overestimate your abilities or underestimate the size of the challenge, you end up failing to prepare or strategize. The risk then is that you are overwhelmed by the challenge and quit prematurely.

First, it's normal to start out any new project of skill acquisition as a beginner. It's part of the process to be a total newbie who doesn't even grasp how much of a newbie they are. That's worth repeating: It's *normal*. If you've identified that you're at this level of your learning, great—there's no shame in it and it's not a mistake. Your task is to maintain open-minded curiosity and energy and be willing to learn (that usually means be willing to make a bit of a fool of yourself).

What you should focus on:

- Enjoy yourself and have fun. Be playful. Don't get in the car with fear and seriousness—remind yourself that learning should feel like exploring, not like a dreaded chore.
- The masters. Identify key players and see what you can learn from them. Don't worry about yourself just yet—focus on what the experts do when they do the task. Look at how people who have been driving for years drive.
- Look for patterns and underlying themes. Ask questions—*a lot* of questions—and be willing to hear a range of different answers.

What you should avoid:

- Being in too much of a hurry to get out of this stage. Being impatient with yourself and judgmental of your beginner's efforts (in fact, as we'll see later, the "beginner's mind" is a pretty powerful place to be)
- Assuming you can be trusted to just know what the next step is. Who knows, maybe you're a brilliant genius who really does know, but in case you're not, be humble and seek guidance about the exact skills you need to be learning and

how to start chipping away at those skills.

The second stage is conscious incompetence. This stage can be a bit of a bummer because, if you've stuck with it, you're suddenly much more aware of just how much it's going to take to gather mastery. In other words, you still don't know how to do the thing, but you're painfully aware of the fact and can see just how big your skill gap is.

Another bit of bad news is that this stage can sometimes last the longest, and that can be a blow to the ego. There's a big difference between a "growth mindset" (i.e., you believe that ability is more like a skill to learn with effort rather than an innate characteristic) and a "fixed mindset" (i.e., you either have the talent or you don't, so there's no point trying to learn anything). The growth mindset is one that will help you navigate this stage with grace and humility, while the fixed mindset is the one that will lead you to giving up before you've reached the goal you wanted to reach. Here, your main task is simply to persist.

What you should focus on:

- Identify a rock-solid source of motivation and tap into it regularly to stay motivated and resilient in the face of setbacks and challenges (more about this later). You keep reminding yourself of why you want to drive and just how great it will be to pass that test and have that freedom.

- Small, achievable goals you can dedicate to yourself daily, or even just hourly if the task is big and intimidating. Forget about highway driving and overtaking and parallel parking; just focus for the moment on one skill: smoothly transitioning from first to second gear. Just do that first.
- Taking action. The previous stage is about more passive learning, whereas this stage is about identifying what you can **do** to get out of your comfort zone, and then committing to doing it.

What you should avoid:

- Comparing yourself to others. You want to pay attention to *how* expert drivers do their thing, but don't turn that into a judgment about yourself. Be inspired by them.
- Being lazy. You need to be patient and put in the work. That's pretty much the long and the short of it. Book your lessons and attend every one, no excuses.

- Having no plan. You need goals, and you need a plan. When (note, not if, but when) your plan goes awry, shrug your shoulders, find the lesson, and move on quickly.

The third stage is conscious competence. Now we're getting somewhere! At some point, all of this patient practice starts to pay off, and you're beginning to make progress. You're improving. It feels amazing to focus on a weakness, work hard at it, and notice that you're gaining ground. Go you! The truth is, though, that at first you might dip in and out of this stage, occasionally falling back into the previous level as you work at retaining your newly acquired skill. So, maybe you're pretty good at driving in the quiet suburbs, but get muddled on busier roads. At this stage you know exactly what competence looks like, and you know when you're hitting that mark . . . and when you're falling short.

What you should focus on:

- Continually refine your skill. Keep going (remember each stage of the deliberate practice roadmap?), and when you mess up, grab hold of it and become curious why.
- Transfer what you're learning to other contexts or situations. Try driving

around a supermarket parking lot. Try driving someone else's car. Try driving an automatic. Drive for longer distances.

- Deliberate, consistent practice that is dynamic enough to change and adapt as you learn.

What to avoid:

- Complacency. Especially with something like driving, it may be perfectly okay to learn the bare minimum to pass your test, and then just get on with life. But be honest with yourself about what you want and are capable of, and don't get lazy when your skill reaches the "good enough" level.
- Avoidance! Sometimes, we can fall into the habit of avoiding our weaker areas in favor of drilling what we already know and are comfortable with. Reverse this tendency and deliberately drill your weaker areas.
- Burning yourself out. You need to take breaks, step back occasionally, and reassess. Some skills need time to settle in and for us to really process them properly. It's a mistake to assume you don't need to pause now and then!

The final stage is unconscious competence.
You've passed your test and have been driving for a year now, and it's all pretty much automatic for you. You know how to drive, but you're not consciously aware of this ability at all times. You'll know you've reached this stage—no matter what skill you're learning—when you can simply use this skill as a tool without skipping a beat. It becomes invisible to you, the way that language is invisible when you're having a very meaty and high-level conversation. There was a time when you were a baby, for example, that you didn't know how to coordinate your legs or even stand up. But, having mastered that skill, you are now able to run, jump, crawl, swim, skip, tiptoe, or do the hokey pokey without giving it a second thought.

Your goal in this stage is to enjoy yourself and revel in your mastery. You could also strive to teach others or develop your practice even further and into different areas—in our example that might look like signing up for an advanced driving course or going on a 4X4 ATV adventure in the deserts of Namibia. Some skills are like "riding a bicycle" and are pretty much banked forever once we learn them, but the more complex ones *do* require some maintenance, so it's worth protecting those gains and embarking on continuous development and refinement.

Perhaps the biggest challenge at this level is accurately identifying exactly how far *you* want to go in this field of mastery. Do you want to be average? Better than average? Expert? Not every skill needs to be pressed to its absolute human limits (can you imagine?), but we should also be on guard against letting fear and laziness trim our dreams down too small. Well-defined goals will allow us to confidently say, "I've done the thing. I can stop now."

Thinking of learning in terms of stages in this way reminds us to not take certain processes for granted, but to continually become aware of where we are, what we're doing, and what we need to do better if we hope to achieve something bigger than that. Before we move on to the next chapter, ask yourself which stage of mastery you might be at (it's possible to straddle two stages). Then identify one thing you can begin to focus on moving forward.

The Zone of Proximal Development

Lev Vygotsky was a Soviet developmental psychologist who was very interested in, amongst other things, the way that human beings acquire skills. In particular, he investigated the way that children learn to do what they do, and what that might imply about human beings in general, not to mention how we might learn better (or, perhaps, *unlearn* when necessary).

Vygotsky proposed his theory of the "zone of proximal development." Traditionally, educational psychologists had always focused on what a child could do at each stage of their development, and how to measure their ability. Vygotsky challenged this and proposed that there are really *two* stages of development that run in parallel:

1. The child's actual level of competence, when tested
2. The child's "potential" level, i.e., what they were capable of when tested with guidance and support from other people or the environment

So, Vygotsky noticed that, for example, Child A would perform at level 5, and Child B would perform at level 6. But when given help and guidance, Child A was able to perform at level 8, while Child B was able to perform at level 7. **The difference between actual competence and potential competence he called the "zone of proximal (or potential) development."** Importantly, this zone varied in size across different children.

Now, this might not seem like such a big deal. Does it matter how much you can do with help? Vygotsky's genius was to notice just what a big difference it does make. In fact, he thought that what a child could do with assistance was a far greater predictor of personal and mental development than what they could do unassisted. As he explained it, what a child can do today with assistance, he can do tomorrow unassisted. In our example, it's actually Child A, who has less initial competence, who will learn and develop the most.

You may have noticed yourself how children take part in this process all the time. When they "play" games of pretend, they always assume the role of someone with far greater competencies than themselves. Identifying with this greater role and carefully monitoring themselves so they emulate it perfectly is precisely how they move from their actual skill level to learning something new.

Role-play (usually of adult characters) requires additional attention, self-awareness, reflection, and adjustment on the part of the child who must continually make sure they remain "in character." As they do so, they learn. We can understand this zone to be the very place where learning occurs. If you only ever do what you already know how to do, then naturally you fail to learn. But if you attempt to do something you cannot even begin to do, even with help, you also fail to learn. You need, as it were, that middle spot where you have mental "training wheels."

In this zone, individuals can learn and acquire new skills with the guidance of a "more knowledgeable other" (MKO), such as a teacher, mentor, or parent. This zone represents the space where learners can progress from basic abilities to more complex tasks, with the support and assistance of someone who possesses greater knowledge and expertise in the subject matter.

Vygotsky's concept highlights the importance of supportive learning *environments* to facilitate effective education and skill development, too. In other words, it's not just people who can guide and support new competencies until they're strong enough to stand on their own. In this second category of support, we can include things like tools and technology of all kinds.

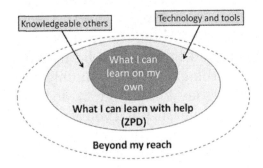

Learning to speak is an example of the ZPD, where children are immersed in an environment with skilled adults who provide constant feedback and various aids (scaffolds) to enhance their verbal communication. Revisiting our stages of mastery from the previous section, we can see how increasing competence also arises in a social context:

1. Unconscious incompetence: you don't know how to tie your shoelaces. Frankly, you don't even understand what shoelaces are for and don't care.
2. Conscious incompetence: everyone at kindergarten is learning to tie shoelaces, and you're suddenly aware that you don't, and it's quite hard.
3. Conscious competence: your mom holds your hands in hers as she slowly

shows you the movements you need to do. Gradually, you mimic her and get better and better at making the knot, till she can take her hands off yours and you can tie the bow yourself. You think that's pretty good.

4. Unconscious competence: you're now middle-aged and tie your shoes literally without thinking about it.

In the above example, your mom's hands on yours are a manifestation of the zone of proximal development. Following her lead, you slowly learn to do it. Had nobody bothered to teach you this skill, chances are you would have taken *a lot* longer to figure it out for yourself. It was against the scaffolding of your mother's skillful help that you tied your own fledgling efforts to at first. Your learning was not so much about your intelligence or creativity, but your ability to work with someone who knew how to do what you were still unable to.

"Scaffolds" can be physical or mental aids, such as using props in yoga or mnemonic devices to remember music staff lines. Fading is then the gradual process of removing these scaffolds (i.e., taking the training wheels off) as individuals become proficient in the skill on their own.

The ZPD is a powerful framework for understanding how we learn best from others and accelerate our progress in various domains. In a way it may seem obvious, but in other ways, it directly challenges many assumptions about how learning works. There is never a clear, sharp line between what we can and can't do. The "growing edge," as it were, is not self-generated, but arises because of *interaction with the social environment*. Genius and raw talent are great things, but the ability to really work well within your ZPD is the true essence of learning.

Here's how to apply the zone of proximal development theory to your practice:

Assess Your Current Position and Learning Style

Determine where you currently stand in terms of knowledge and skills, and identify the areas you want to improve. Understand how you learn best—whether it's through modeling, detailed instructions, hands-on practice, etc. You may not even have this insight yet, in which case a teacher or mentor will be particularly helpful.

For instance, if you're trying to be a better cook, start by evaluating your current cooking abilities. Identify the types of dishes you can already cook confidently and those that might be a "step up" from your current level. Next consider how you prefer to learn cooking skills—whether you learn best by following written recipes, watching video tutorials, or having someone demonstrate the cooking process for you.

Seek out a More Knowledgeable Other (MKO)

Look for someone who possesses expertise in the skills you want to develop. This could be a teacher, a tutor, a peer, an expert, or even online tutorials. Communicate your preferred learning style to the MKO and seek their guidance and support in acquiring new skills.

For instance, engage with your chosen MKO or resource to learn new cooking skills and recipes. Pay attention to their instructions, techniques, and tips. Use their skill to bootstrap your own. As you try out new recipes, follow along with the guidance provided. It's essential to have a learning-oriented mindset, embrace mistakes as part of the learning process, and be open to feedback and improvement. If instead your mindset is fixed ("I'll only ever know what I know now") and you find errors and corrections humiliating, you'll be passing up on the precious chance to learn more quickly and more effectively.

Test and Apply the New Skill Independently

After working with the MKO, practice the new skill on your own. Assess whether you have internalized the instructions and feedback received during the learning process. If you feel confident and capable of applying the skill independently, you have successfully progressed within your zone of proximal development. Continue this process of learning, seeking new MKOs, and advancing your skills.

After cooking the new meals with the guidance of the MKO or resource, evaluate your results and assess your learning. Ask yourself if you have successfully internalized the techniques and instructions. Are you now able to cook the dish independently? If you feel confident and satisfied with your cooking, you have effectively advanced within your zone of proximal development for cooking that particular dish. Congratulations! Crack out the wine and enjoy it.

The Yerkes–Dodson Law

A closely related principle is called the Yerkes–Dodson law. Even if you're not familiar with this term, however, you've probably experienced it firsthand in your own life. An example will illustrate the idea neatly:

Tyler has just landed his first job out of college and is thrilled. He's pretty nervous, but the pressure seems to fire him up and he's full of energy for the first few months, loving the new challenge and feeling inspired to push out of his comfort zone a little. Life is good. He's learning new things constantly, rising to challenges, and earning a name for himself. After a year he is promoted. He can't believe his luck. Everyone around him admires how much he is thriving. That beautiful state of mind called "flow"? He's in it all day, every day.

In a year's time he gets promoted again, this time to a formidable role known for making high demands on people. More than anyone Tyler knows the value of pushing yourself, though, so despite his apprehension, he accepts the new position. This time it feels different, though. It quickly becomes clear that the challenge alone is no longer energizing him. He is genuinely lost at times and starts making pretty big mistakes. Things start to feel rushed and out of his control. He isn't even sure who to tell that he's struggling, or how they would even help him. In fact, each new demand seems to just fill him with dread.

He doesn't get it: he loves this field, he loves his work, and he used to be inspired by challenge. These days he wakes up and thinks, "I'm actually a big fraud and a loser. Clearly I can't do this thing. It's just too hard."

What happened? Well, according to psychologists Robert Yerkes and John Dodson, Tyler is simply experiencing a particularly skewed ratio of arousal (that's stress, to you and me) and performance.

The theory, first put forward in 1908, is based on experiments with rats motivated by electric shocks to escape a maze. The "inverted-U curve" graphically represents the relationship between their arousal state and their performance, showing that performance actually improves with moderate pressure, reaches a peak, *and then declines if pressure becomes too high or too low.* This is what happened to poor Tyler. He was a rat who found the sweet spot—but then went beyond it and experienced a drop in performance.

According to the theory, peak performance occurs when the level of pressure matches the task's demands.

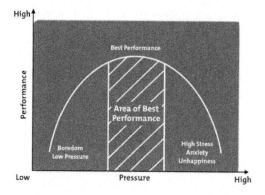

We tend to imagine that the world would be great with zero stress, but this is not quite true—some stress is useful, since it motivates and inspires us (otherwise there'd be no such thing as fun competition, right?). When **pressure is too low**, people lack motivation and may approach their work in a lazy manner. Basically, they get bored—this is the area to the far left of the graph, where pressure is low and so is performance.

In contrast, when **pressure is too high** it overwhelms people, rather than inspires them. Their performance drops off as they feel anxious, rushed, intimidated, confused, or that awful sense of dread that Tyler felt. It's easy to see why—faced with a task that is so difficult you know you couldn't possibly crack it, what else would you feel but a sense of defeat?

The middle of the curve represents the optimal state where individuals are both

51

motivated by pressure and yet not overloaded, enabling them to experience "flow," a highly productive and enjoyable state of work. Achieving this balance is key to achieving one's personal best. There are two big insights from this observation:

1. Stress is helpful—provided it's at the right level
2. While struggling at a task is often a result of the demand being too great and "arousal" being too high, you can just as well experience poor performance because *you're not stressed enough*.

You've probably spotted the overlap between this diagram and the zone of proximal development. Our area of best performance is analogous to the zone of proximal development—we fare better when challenges are just beyond our capabilities, but not massively so. A big mistake Tyler could make now, however, is to decide he's burnt out and overstressed, and completely turn down the demand on himself. He would then overshoot and find himself in the boredom zone—and again underperforming.

We see again that optimal learning, growth, and development are never a one-size-fits-all solution, and our best approach is likely to change over time, just as we change and our needs and blind spots change, too. Sometimes the best tactic will be to increase the challenge; sometimes the best tactic will be to do the exact opposite. You may start out doing things a certain way, and it may genuinely work—but that doesn't mean you should stick to that strategy forever.

The Yerkes–Dodson law goes on to identify four key influencers of this overall relationship between arousal/stress and performance:

1. Skill level
2. Personality
3. Trait anxiety
4. Task complexity

This is a big deal: What counts as "stress" for you may not seem that way to someone else, and experts will have different challenges and experiences to beginners. Furthermore, context is obviously a big part of it, and so is the skill complexity and difficulty—i.e., are you talking about tying shoelaces or building software for a particle accelerator?

Skill level influences performance and may require adjusting pressure to maintain engagement. Personality also plays a role, with extroverts potentially performing better in high-pressure situations, while introverts may thrive with less pressure. Trait anxiety, or a person's self-talk, can impact performance, with confident individuals better able to handle pressure (they tend to have a bigger zone of proximal development because their guiding "teacher" is actually their own inner voice coaching them through—something to think about!). Task complexity affects how individuals respond to pressure, with simple tasks being more suitable for higher pressure and complex tasks benefiting from a calmer environment.

To use insights from this "law," consider the following tips:

Align Practice Sessions with Your Energy Levels

Pay attention to your energy patterns and identify when you feel most alert and focused. Schedule your practice sessions during these peak energy times. This will enable you to make the most of your cognitive abilities and enhance your learning experience. Reserve periods of low energy for lighter tasks or breaks, allowing you to recharge. Don't forget, also, to schedule the most challenging task at the *beginning* of your peak energy zone.

Find the Optimal Challenge Level

Understand that practicing a new skill requires finding the right balance between difficulty and your current abilities. For simpler aspects of the skill or tasks you've already mastered, challenge yourself by increasing the complexity or speed. On the other hand, for more intricate or challenging aspects, slow down and break them down into smaller, manageable steps. Adjusting the challenge level to match your current proficiency will help you stay engaged and make steady progress.

Manage Stress and Avoid Extremes

Recognize that too much stress or pressure can hinder your learning process, while too little can lead to complacency or lack of motivation. Maintain a healthy level of challenge that stretches your abilities without overwhelming you. Be aware of signs of stress or burnout and take regular breaks to relax and recharge. Utilize stress management techniques, such as mindfulness exercises or positive self-talk, to keep stress levels in check and maintain a positive mindset during your skill practice.

Finally, one of the worst things you can do when working with both your aspirations and your limitations is to *incorrectly ascribe difficulty to your innate core self*. What this might mean is that you push yourself beyond your zone of competence, fail, and then immediately self-criticize and conclude that you're stupid and can't do it. Instead, get neutral and get curious: If you slow down or ease up on the complexity, does the task become easier? At what point are things manageable, and when do they tip over into being unmanageable? By the same token, don't find yourself experiencing boredom and immediately conclude that the task is worthless or uninteresting. Dial up the challenge a notch first and observe your reaction.

Summary:

- To learn effectively, you need more than talent. You need a solid plan of attack, the right mindset, and plenty of contingency planning—i.e., you need to learn how to learn.
- Not all practice is created equal. There are three types: naive, purposeful, and deliberate practice, the latter being most effective. This is where we act deliberately in a well-defined field with clear distinctions between experts and novices, with a skilled coach providing tailored practice strategies and feedback.

- The deliberate practice roadmap is a reiterative spiral: It begins with finding a teacher, then entails assessing your limits, setting SMART goals, focused practice, and feedback . . . and then it repeats.
- Slow practice is practicing a sequence at a slower tempo first and gradually increasing the speed to reach the desired performance level.
- Energy isn't infinite; we need to be strategic to make the best use of it. Energy tends to be higher at the start of a session, so practice the more challenging tasks first. Aim for skills that are about five to ten percent above the current maximum skill level. Be willing to push outside your comfort zone.
- Learning proceeds through four stages: unconscious incompetence, conscious incompetence, conscious competence, and unconscious competence—pitch your efforts according to the needs and skills of the level you're at.
- The difference between actual competence and potential competence is called the "zone of proximal development," where you can achieve with the help of a more knowledgeable

other. Working within this sweet spot can help you optimize your practice.

- The Yerkes–Dodson law shows that performance improves with moderate pressure, reaches a peak, but declines if pressure becomes too high or too low. Try to find the optimal stress and challenge level, which may change over time.

Part 2: You Need the Right Mindset

Cultivate a Beginner's Mind

You've got a roadmap to developing mastery, a structure for *how* you learn and develop.

Now let's look at the best attitude and state of mind you can adopt to make your use of that map the best it can be.

Once there was a famous Zen monk who was known to be an expert of the Buddhist text, the "diamond sutra." In fact, he was the only one in his region to even own a copy of this rare and expensive book, and he carried it with him everywhere he went. People from far and wide would come to consult with this wise man, and benefit from his knowledge about this important Buddhist text. He was so good at dispensing wisdom from this book that soon ordinary people in his region came to understand its contents, too.

One day the monk approached a woman in the market who was selling tea and cake. The monk was hungry and wanted some but had no money to pay. So he told her, "I'm carrying with me a book of incredible value and power—the diamond sutra. If you give me some of your tea and cake, I'll show this treasure of perfect knowledge."

In fact, the woman was no stranger to the teachings in the diamond sutra, and made a countersuggestion to the monk. She said, "Wise monk, if you only answer me a simple question, I'll give you as much tea and cake as you want." The hungry monk agreed. The woman asked her question: "What do you eat cakes with? With the mind of the past, the mind of the present, or the mind of the future?"

The monk thought about this for a while. He couldn't answer. He brought out his diamond sutra and consulted it. In fact he ended up reading it for some time, and soon it was late and the woman had to pack up her tea and cake stall for the day.

"Turns out you're not so wise after all," she said to the monk.

"But what is the answer?" he said as he watched her pack up and leave.

"The answer is that you eat cakes with your *mouth*," she said, and left him hungry.

The moral of this story is clear: Sometimes we can "know" so much that our minds are closed to knowing anything else . . . including something new and something true. **The "paradox" of expertise is that when we know (or just think we know), we are immediately in a smaller, more closed, and more limited frame of mind**. The monk had great knowledge—but of one thing. Everything he encountered was passed through that lens. Being an expert at the diamond sutra made him feel as though he *already had* the answer.

The clever woman guessed this and challenged him. Her question was just a nonsense question—but it did reveal that the monk, in all his wisdom, was unable to see the obvious.

It really is a paradox. To learn, we approach the unknown with humility, curiosity, and a certain emptiness. Thus, we learn. But once we have learned, our minds close as we become more sure, less inquisitive, and even arrogant. Thus, we fail to learn. This is why it's often the case that lauded experts sometimes fail to truly comprehend paradigm-shifting changes in their field—they are not paying attention. Instead, some young and inexpert beginner comes in and sees something new, solves the problem, or identifies the secret that was there all along. The expert is good at many things, but he's not good at being simple, being obvious and, most importantly, at saying, "I don't know."

The great Krishnamurti once said of a beginner's mind,

> "There is no movement of learning when there is the acquisition of knowledge; the two are incompatible, they are contradictory. The movement of learning implies a state in which the mind has no previous experience stored up as knowledge. The mind that is learning is an **innocent mind**, whereas the mind that is merely acquiring knowledge is old, stagnant, corrupted by the past. An innocent mind perceives instantly, it is learning all the time without accumulating, and such a mind alone is mature."

The term "beginner's mind" or "Shoshin" originates from Japanese Zen Buddhism and refers to the idea that as we become more knowledgeable about a subject, we may become close-minded and limit our ability to learn further. Shunryu Suzuki's book *Zen Mind, Beginner's Mind* first popularized this concept in the West, saying, **"In the beginner's mind there are many possibilities, but in the expert's there are few."**

Some years back, geneticists were transfixed with the idea of sequencing the human genome. The field had been asking some powerful questions for years: What do genes tell us about how disease develops? At the time, Bill Clinton called the Human Genome Project "the most important, most wondrous map ever produced by humankind," an achievement somewhat on par with putting a man on the moon. This "book of life" was much hyped, and when it was complete, it was assumed it would revolutionize the medical field and change humankind's relationship with disease and mortality forever more.

That didn't happen. The project cost almost three billion dollars and ultimately revealed that the human genome had about the same number of genes as a fruit fly or mouse, and *three times less* than an onion. Why was the project such a disappointment? The answers are complicated, but one aspect is that genetic experts were seeing a range of questions using a very narrow set of assumptions and prior knowledge—their version of the diamond sutra, so to speak. As knowledgeable educated experts, they had begun to ask, "What gene causes XYZ disease?" and had stopped asking the question they asked when they were beginners: "What causes disease, anyway?"

Everyone knows that people are more complex than onions (some of them, anyway), and so they were forced to conclude that there was a lot that their "book of life" didn't cover. The project wasn't a failure, but it did highlight certain assumptions—the kind of assumptions that only very educated people held! Today, biologists are beginning to concede that the development of disease is complex and down to many interacting variables, genetics being just one of them. Of course, any woman selling cake in a market could have told them that in the first place!

Embracing a Beginner's Mind involves more than just being open-minded—it's a total stance of receptivity, curiosity, ambiguity, even playfulness. It's having a fundamental respect for reality as it is, before and outside of what you have already decided about it. It is a recognition that, paradoxically, knowledge comes from the willingness to embrace total ignorance, and that too much "knowing" can actually make a person profoundly unwise.

Developing a beginner's mind means letting go of preconceived notions and expectations about outcomes, which reduces the risk of stress and disappointment as a nice side effect. This is akin to meditation, where one approaches each session with openness, avoiding expectations and judgments. Everything that has come before is set aside, in order for the present moment, as it is, to be encountered in an "innocent" way—new, raw, and fundamentally unknown. Observing thoughts without comment or judgment and simply letting them go is a central aspect of this practice.

The principles of a beginner's mind extend beyond meditation into daily life. By being open, receptive, and curious, we can tap into deeper creativity, flexibility, and resilience to face challenges more effectively. It is about being *new* in each moment—and allowing that moment to be free of whatever came before. It's the place where learning becomes inevitable.

Here's how a beginner's mind can help you in your practice:

Don't Assume

Sometimes, you grasp an idea or concept on an intellectual level, and so you content yourself with the feeling that you *know* it. But do you really? Often we feel as though we have full comprehension of some skill or piece of knowledge, whereas in reality we are just familiar with it. To really test if you've actually learned something, try to explain the idea or concept to someone else out loud. This will immediately show you where you're making assumptions and taking mental shortcuts. Have you ever read a book, thought you understood it, and then when someone asked you what it was about, you drew a blank and couldn't really say?

It's only human to be a little overconfident in your knowledge, especially if it was hard won! But beware that this can lead to closed-mindedness. When you try to explain something to someone else, you'll reveal any conceptual or logical gaps you might have overlooked. This is especially true if what you "know" is more akin to an argument or philosophical position; it's only when you test drive the argument in real conversation that you can see whether it holds its own or not. Get into the habit of asking what you *don't* know and what you're *not* thinking of.

Seek Out Counterevidence

As you gather more and more knowledge, you can inadvertently set up a kind of confirmation bias for yourself, and a "filter bubble" where you only permit yourself to encounter material that agrees with what you already know. This is why old and established companies can sometimes perform so poorly against relative newcomers to the industry— they were so busy doing what they'd always done, they weren't paying attention to what they weren't doing. Their competitors were, however!

Again, it's only human to want to seek out knowledge that is consistent with what we already know. From the moment we're born, we erect frameworks of meaning onto which we graft every new experience—and that means that even when we see something new, we are already in the process of determining how it might be just like something we've seen before. It's the old "when you have a hammer, everything looks like a nail." When you have a certain framework of knowledge and understanding, you mysteriously seem to encounter problems and situations that perfectly fit that framework.

Assume that confirmation bias will happen by default, unless you consciously choose to be aware and challenge it. One excellent way of doing that is to deliberately seek out information that doesn't correspond to your existing frameworks or confirm your existing conclusions. You don't need to wait for someone to argue with you—argue with yourself. Assume the "other side" has a good point and argue on their behalf. When you go online to search for information, search for it as someone who has the *opposite* of your beliefs or knowledge base would. Then engage with it with as much intellectual honesty and integrity as you can. You may find you were totally "right." But chances are you'll learn something new.

Reframe Knowledge and Skill as Something Malleable

Here's our old friend again, the growth mindset. The best attitude is where you understand that intelligence and knowledge are not special gifts conferred on a lucky few at birth, but rather something you can actively, purposely grow. Intelligence and knowledge can be accrued—and potentially lost.

What this means is that one day, when you learn something valuable or bank a skill, you are not *finished*. You cannot sit down and say that, from here on out, you know and understand, and that's that. If you do so, you shut yourself off from the true source of growth and learning. In the same vein, don't look at eminent and accomplished experts and assume that they are wise and superior and all-knowing, while you are not and never can be. True, there is such a thing as "talent" in this world—but it matters less than you think.

Invite Awe

Little children know nothing—and the world is beautiful for them. They are astonished by *everything*. Any event is a source of wonder and amazement for them, and any path of exploration is taken to be as worthy as any other. They are playful, curious, and unassuming. They do not grab hold of knowledge and understanding as something they *own*. They are simply awash in the wonder of being alive in this incredible universe—and their joy is what's in the front of their mind, not their pride or vanity at having figured something out.

There's a reason the old professor archetype is usually someone who is jaded and cynical. This dry, tired person has seen it all and is singularly unimpressed. You show them a beautiful flower and they say, "Ah yes, *Campanula rotundifolia.* Very common."

Instead, cultivate awe—which is a kind of respectful humility in the face of the grandeur of nature. Seek out and immerse yourself in wonder, and not in the smugness that comes with believing you have found some conceptual container to keep that wonder in. Gaze up at the night sky, listen to stirring music that makes language look about a thousand times too small, or simply play. There are so many things to learn—don't allow most of them to be hidden from you because you were convinced you'd already mastered the curriculum!

"Away From" Versus "Toward" Motivation

Naturally, you reach a point at which "playing" peters out and you're no longer, shall we say, in awe of your daily practice session. Frankly, you're facing a session that proves to be a bit of a grind. What now?

A beginner's mind is great, but it's not enough on its own.

You also need, drumroll, *motivation*.

But motivation is one of those words most of us use without really understanding what we're talking about. People say "Follow your passion," but they also say "Just do it." Which is the right way?

There are *two* main types of motivation: "away-from" motivation and "toward" motivation. "Away-from" motivation involves avoiding something undesirable, while "toward" motivation revolves around striving toward a goal. *Both* types can be beneficial, but an imbalance can lead to issues.

There are a few questions emerging here:

Is one style more appropriate to the particular task you're doing?

Is one style preferable to you personally?

Is one style more fitting for the stage of development you're at?

We are all different, and we are all motivated by different things and in different ways. Your "motivation style" reflects your own character and personality, but also your unique goals and priorities. Even then, what motivates you in one sphere or stage of life may no longer motivate you as you change and develop, or the context changes.

Consider this example. Jenny is morbidly obese, and doctors have warned her that she won't be able to undergo the life-saving operation she needs unless she loses drastic amounts of weight. Without the operation, her chances of survival are slim. *That's* one hell of a motivation. Jenny is experiencing very stark "away-from" motivation—losing weight will allow her to get away from the very real threat of dying. So, because her life depended on it, literally, Jenny lost the weight. She got the operation. Her life continued.

Then she started piling weight back on again . . .

Somehow, losing weight now is harder than it was before. Her motivation has changed.

Her (mean) mother says to her, "Come on, you don't want to end up back there again, do you?" But somehow, this focus on the negative just doesn't motivate Jenny anymore—in fact it stresses and depresses her. One day, Jenny bumps into an old friend at the local swimming pool. Her friend has been on a massive fitness kick and now looks like a million bucks. Jenny can't deny it: She's jealous. All at once, she finds herself with a new goal: "I want to look that good." The very next day she signs up at a gym—something she never thought she would do.

Now, this is not to say that either of Jenny's motivations are good or bad; rather, *what works* is liable to change over time. If we want to be effective, we have to notice what works for us and why.

"Toward" motivation focuses on positive aspirations—like looking smoking hot in a bikini. It would be a mistake to think that this is a better form of motivation, however. It's not. Whether you avoid something you don't want or move toward something you do is irrelevant if, ultimately, you're motivating yourself in the way you want to be motivated.

Humans *are* generally more motivated to move away from negative outcomes than toward positive ones. This fear of loss often leads to conservative decision-making and a preference for maintaining the status quo rather than taking risks to advance. There is nothing really wrong with acting to avoid an unwanted future outcome, and it's an appropriate motivation when it comes to something like using contraception or taking out travel insurance. Plus, before they learn to regulate themselves and act with enough foresight into the future, the only way their parents can get them to do something is to use this kind of motivation.

However, the only thing this type of motivation can do for you is help you avoid that outcome. That's it. In saying what you don't want, you are no closer to identifying or moving toward what you do want. Jenny was motivated to lose enough weight so she could get her operation—but no more than that. The doctors didn't tell her she needed to be a fitness model, only that she needed to drop enough weight so that the surgery wouldn't be too risky. That's the problem with this kind of motivation: It will motivate you only just enough to avoid the bad thing—it cannot make you excellent.

Running away from something works, but it fundamentally contradicts the way that natural talents practice.

People who practice effectively and achieve a degree of excellence are seldom motivated by their desire to escape something. Rather, they have a keen vision of what they're moving toward, and they focus on developing skills that push them beyond their current abilities. Their actions are aspirational, hopeful, and future oriented.

"Lose a bunch of weight or you'll die" lends itself well to "away-from" motivation . . . but it's not the kind of thing that will help you become a concert pianist, pass the bar exam, or become an accomplished trapeze artist. For that you need a vision.

Make Your Goals Positive

Not positive in content, but *grammatically* positive—i.e., don't state what you don't want; state what you do want. What are you building, striving for, wanting? When setting great goals, use positive, toward wording instead of negative, away-from wording. For example, instead of saying your goal is to "not mess up my speech," reframe it to "deliver my speech with confidence." Sometimes, your goals may naturally be more focused on specific problems you have in life, but even still, try not to focus on the problem and how much you don't like it, but on the alternative situation you're trying to create.

Mix It Up

Use both forms of motivation in how you achieve your goal—a little stick, a little carrot. Away-from motivation can serve as an initial catalyst for action, initiating the journey toward the goal. However, to maintain momentum and prevent stagnation, a strong toward motivation may come in handy. Likewise, you might use a future, positive orientation to identify the long-range goals you want, but use more away-from motivation in the day to day. For example, you ultimately want to pass the bar exam because you have ambitions for your career and the work you want to do in the world. But day to day, you might work through your to-do list with nothing more to motivate you than the fact that your partner will hassle you if you don't, or you'll feel guilty if you procrastinate.

There may be one or two course modules you hate, and even though they're not really necessary, you have no choice but to do them. They're part of your broader goal, but the real reason you do them is basically because that broader goal is essentially held hostage: Pass these boring modules *or else you'll jeopardize the thing you really care about.* Another example: You may be genuinely motivated to build a new business, but that doesn't mean you really care about, say, setting up your taxes or hiring an accountant. You'll do it, but to be honest, your motivation is mostly wanting to avoid getting in trouble!

Set Interim Goals

Break down your main goal into smaller, manageable interim goals. Each step toward the goal provides a sense of accomplishment and positive reinforcement. Setting interim goals helps maintain motivation and prevents becoming overwhelmed by the larger end goal.

To really make the concept of interim goals work for you, however, you have to think of each mini goal in terms of motivation. Deliberately pause after each advance you make and do two things:

1. Zoom out and check to see how far you've come, where you are now on your "map," and whether you need to make any adjustments.
2. Celebrate! Really notice that you have moved one notch further to what you want (or even one notch further away from what you don't want) and let that sink in.

Sometimes, the idea of "baby steps" can feel intimidating: "It's hard enough having one goal; now you're asking me to have twelve?!" One important part of using interim goals, however, is to cut down on overwhelm and bootstrap your motivation onto a goal that is a little closer and easier to see. Use broad vision to map out a path, then put your head down and tackle those tasks one at a time. When you're doing a task, all you have to do is think about that task. That's all. Nothing else.

You don't have to think about the next task in line or the one after that. Just this one. When you've completed it, pause to check where you are, adjust if necessary, celebrate, then dive back in and do the next task. This way, you get the best of both: a big-picture vision to keep you going, but also a small enough vision to stop you from getting overwhelmed.

Friedman's Ways to Make the Most Out of Practice

"Practice doesn't make perfect. Perfect practice makes perfect."

You've probably heard that quote somewhere before, right? It's a great piece of advice, and it reminds us that it's worth picking apart our assumptions about this vague word "practice" to get to the heart of what we're really trying to do when we attempt to master a new skill.

A while back, it became fashionable to think of your cardiovascular fitness in terms of steps. If you could achieve the magical number of ten thousand steps every day, you could enjoy good heart health, lose weight, and all the rest. Without thinking too much about where this "rule" came from or its underlying rationale (why ten thousand, exactly? What about 9,998 steps? What counts as a step, anyway?), people got to work getting those steps in no matter what. They tracked steps with apps and gadgets, entered step competitions with colleagues, and found themselves obsessively wondering how many steps they racked up walking to the kitchen or checking the mailbox.

Similarly, Malcolm Gladwell's book *Outliers: The Story of Success* proposed the very same number—ten thousand—as the number of hours of practice required to become a master performer in any particular area. Cue the world frantically calculating how many hours of accordion practice or oil painting or Jiu Jitsu they have to squeeze in if they hope to achieve mastery before they die. By the way, in case you're curious, if you practiced an hour a day every single day for the rest of your life, it would take *more than twenty-seven years* to rack up your ten thousand hours. Ouch.

The good news is, you don't have to walk ten thousand steps a day, and you don't need to commit ten thousand hours of practice to master any skill. The book was inspired in part by research by Ericsson and colleagues, who investigated the progress of violin students at a Berlin music academy and discovered that the best performers had put in around 7400 hours of practice before age eighteen, and around ten thousand hours by the time they were twenty.

But does this really tell us anything useful about the nature of mastery?

There are a few problems with the idea of thinking that it's purely the amount of time you invest that counts. You should be able to guess the problem by now: Not all practice is created equal. An hour by a beginner tuba player is not the same as an hour by an advanced software developer learning a new programming language. An intense hour where you're supported by a mentor who is spotting and correcting errors in real time is not the same as an hour of aimless repetition of things you already know to do.

So, **quantity doesn't matter, quality does—** i.e., "perfect practice" and a deliberate strategy is what moves you forward, not clocking hours.

If you're in the gym and trying to master a particular lift, you may need a trainer at your side to constantly check and correct your form, suggest adjustments, spur you on when you're being lazy, and slow you down if you're rushing. But deliberate practice is just as much about what happens outside the gym and inside your head. So, when we talk about quality practice, we're not just talking about your technique playing the violin or doing a deadlift or mastering that triple pirouette. Your perfect practice also includes the maintenance of the right mindset.

In his book *Decoding Greatness: How the Best in the World Reverse Engineer Success*, Ron Friedman provides strategies for enhancing implementation, which involve effective practice, performance measurement, and managing the risks necessary for learning and growth. While it may seem obvious that practice is essential for improvement, Friedman emphasizes that practicing incorrectly or inefficiently can be a common pitfall. Incorrect and ineffectual practice can mean a poor technique, but it can also mean a poor attitude. To optimize your efforts and avoid wasting time, he presents several guidelines for practicing effectively.

Reflect

Unless you're at school, you're probably going to have to be an adult and take charge of your own learning process. That means monitoring your performance, keeping track of your goals, and continually adjusting your strategy as you go. In other words, you cannot be passive.

Ask yourself:

What's working and what's not working?

What's the one thing I could do right now that would instantly make things easier/better?

Am I doing anything that's not really necessary or essential? Can I drop it?

Get in the habit of comparing before and afters—not to judge or condemn yourself, but to keep a keen eye on how you're advancing and why. Take note where you are at the beginning of a practice session, and where you are at the end. Take one day a week where you review your progress and set new goals for yourself. Once a month or even once a year, take a moment to see what you've achieved, what you haven't, and what you can do now to address those gaps.

A journal is a great way to keep track of all this data, but wherever possible, assign numbers to the data you're gathering so you can accurately measure and quantify your progress (or lack thereof). Doing so allows you to see broader patterns you might have missed otherwise. For example, you might start to notice over the course of a few months that your performance is always worse on a Monday. You investigate and realize that you tend to stay up late on Sunday evenings, and you're too tired to make the best use of your practice sessions early the next morning. So you change up your schedule. Perhaps you notice that when you make your practice sessions shorter, you actually end up achieving more and feeling more positive about your gains. You decide to experiment by making them even shorter and see what happens.

Challenge Yourself

According to Friedman, **the real value of practice is not to keep rehearsing at the same level, but to constantly be pushing up against your current skill and comfort level**. There is a Greek story about a mighty warrior called Milo who lived in the sixth century BC. He was a celebrated athlete and wrestler, and renowned for his unique training regimen. It was said that Milo started his training by carrying a newborn calf on his shoulders a certain distance. The next day, he picked up the same calf and repeated the task. He did this every day after, but of course, as the calf slowly grew, so did his strength. At last, Milo was able to carry a fully grown bull on his shoulders.

In fitness and weight training circles, Milo's story is often used to illustrate the principle of *progressive overload*. The idea is to never stagnate at a fixed, comfortable level, but to be constantly challenging yourself, even if just in tiny increments. In the gym, this looks like gradually increasing the weight, reps, or sets you complete of a certain exercise, or decreasing the recovery time between exercises. But the principle can be applied to other forms of practice, too.

If your practice gets too repetitive or easy, you're not really learning anything (well, except perhaps how to repeat an easy thing!). This can creep up on you very quickly if you're not vigilant. For example, you may set yourself a challenge to master two hundred new vocabulary words in the language you're learning, and then achieve this goal. You may be so proud of yourself and so keen to enjoy your new achievement that you waste quite a lot of time drilling and revisiting those same vocabulary words—instead of learning new ones.

The moment you find something easy, that's a signal for you to check to see if you can dial things up a notch. Stay in the learning zone, not the "happily coasting" zone. That might mean, for example, identifying the three out of ten most challenging math questions in a practice paper, and deciding to make them the focus of your study session that day, rather than devoting all your time to the remaining seven that you have already mastered and find pretty easy.

Ask yourself:

Can I do more?

Is there anywhere I'm being complacent?

What difficult next step might I be avoiding?

Mentally Rehearse

If you're thinking creatively, the definition of "practice" can include lots of different things.

Mental rehearsal and purposeful visualization are extremely powerful—and it's an approach that many of the world's greats have used to their advantage. In 1972, Suinn et al. published a study showing that the muscles in the legs of competitive skiers were activated almost to the same degree when they were *imagining* skiing as when they were actually doing it. That's a pretty startling finding—it strongly suggests that mental rehearsal is almost as valuable as physically going through the motions.

Now, in fairness, the astonishing results of this study have yet to be replicated to this extent, but this hasn't stopped many professional skiers—not to mention golfers, runners, swimmers, etc.—from using mental rehearsal themselves. It may be that imaginal rehearsal works because of its overall effects on the central nervous system, and helps people mentally and psychologically prepare and self-regulate. Whatever the mechanism, it's worth exploring whether this form of "practice" can be useful for you.

It's easy to do, only it takes a little time and focus. As if you were meditating, go quiet in yourself, still your body and breath, and then try to conjure a vivid "picture" in your mind (it doesn't have to literally be an image, by the way, but should be multisensory and include thoughts and emotions, too).

Depending on the goals you're trying to achieve, **carefully imagine the time, place, sensory details, and nuances of a scene you're rehearsing**. Maybe it's a music recital or other performance, a test, or simply a scenario in which you overcome your current challenges. Mental imagery helps you de-stress and focus, "troubleshoot," and lock down important details of previous learning. However, avoid focusing on success imagery, as it can lead to complacency and hinder performance. Practice is about *how* you get there—focusing on the point where you're already there may feel nice, but it's unlikely to be useful in any way.

For example, prior to running a marathon, mentally rehearse how you might move through each training session leading up to the big day. Flesh it out in your mind's eye. See possible obstacles (for example, skipping sessions) and rehearse exactly what you'll do when the temptation arises, and how you'll get around it. Picture yourself waking up every morning and the exact sequence of events you'll follow to get out there on the road. Dwell on the feeling of the shoelaces in your hand, the chillness of the air outside. In your mind, rehearse the self-talk "I can do this. One step at a time, I can do it." Perhaps as you run through this "movie" in your mind again and again, you start to connect it with positive emotions such as pride, determination, and a feeling of invincibility. In your imagination, you see yourself smiling as you head out the door, knowing that for today, you've conquered your fear and laziness.

The next morning, when you wake up, you do the routine exactly as you imagined it first in your mind. Mental rehearsal is great for drilling the actual tasks you are trying to master—for example, mentally running through guitar fingering sequences while you're riding the subway, or quietly practicing a speech in your head as you shower. But, as you can see with the marathon example, it's also useful for rehearsing attitudes, ways of coping, and techniques for overcoming challenges.

Create an Alter Ego

Natalie is a shy person. She's also dead funny and has wanted to be a standup comedian for as long as she can remember. She spends two hours every Thursday evening at a local comedy club, where she perfects her routine at an open mic night. Over the years, she's polished her unique voice and her content to such a degree that she regularly gets standing ovations. A fan approaches her after a particularly successful show and is filled with praise for Natalie.

"How do you do that?" says the fan. "You're so confident. I wish I was that brave. The thing is, I'm really, really shy."
"Yeah," says Natalie. "So am I."
"You are? But you don't *seem* shy. How can you get up there on that stage when you feel shy?"
"Well, *I* can't. But I created another version of myself who can."

Natalie explains that every Thursday evening, she actually takes on the role of an entirely different persona—Naomi. This Naomi is calm and witty and oozes charm and likeability. Where Natalie feels self-conscious about performing, Naomi actually seeks out the limelight and thrives in it. Where Natalie is worried about whether she'll make a fool of herself, Naomi purposefully tries to make a fool of herself—and entertain her audience in the process.

Natalie has discovered the power of having an alter ego (from the Latin for "other self"), which is a well-known technique that performers of all stripes have used for decades. You don't need to be a comedian to benefit from this technique, though. **Developing your own personalized alter ego is a powerful strategy to bridge the gap between your current ability and your aspired level of competence**, whether it's with public speaking, sports, languages, instruments, or something else.

Remember Vygotsky and the zone of proximal development? Well, the act of assuming the role of someone who is more skillful than yourself is really just a way of being *your own* MKO—more knowledgeable other. When you pretend to be your alter ego, what you are doing is using their identity as a set of training wheels for your own behavior:

1. You recognize your own limited skills
2. You imagine someone else who doesn't have those limitations
3. You imagine what they would do
4. You act "as if" you are them, and do what they would do

5. It feels phony at first (after all, it's just acting), but soon, you seem to really identify with the role
6. At some point, you are no longer acting. You *are* that role
7. Standing ovation

Effective parents use this technique when they want to help their children master some new skill. They say, "I know you're afraid of getting your shot, but imagine you're Batman. He would be brave and strong, wouldn't he? Let's pretend we're Batman when we go to the clinic today and see if you can be brave and strong like him."

Natalie essentially did the same thing. "I know you're shy and afraid of standing up on stage, but imagine you're already a totally amazing performer, someone called, I don't know, Naomi. She would just strut out there and own the stage, wouldn't she? Let's pretend we're her and see if we can mimic some of that self-confidence."

By embodying this alter ego, you can tap into new qualities and strengths that might otherwise be inaccessible because of self-doubt. You might always think that a certain desired behavior is out there, something that belongs to other people, something you could never have or be. When you make-believe that you are your alter ego, those qualities are brought much closer to your world and into your self-concept. It's like a self-induced placebo—you step out of your comfort zone and actually *do* perform at that higher level. It's an interesting philosophical question: What really is the difference between pretending to be competent and actually being competent? Meanwhile, your psyche is busy adjusting itself and resolving the discrepancy—it starts to believe its own act. The advice to "fake it until you make it," then, turns out to be solid gold.

You may get stumped by obstacles and adversities—but as long as you can imagine that your alter ego doesn't, you can see a way forward.

You may find certain tasks almost impossible, but if you can imagine an alter ego who finds them easy, you can start to believe that they are possible and exactly how you might make a bit of progress.

You may feel lazy, afraid, resentful, confused, or anything else, but if you can imagine that your alter ego doesn't feel that way, you open up the possibility of slowly shifting your mindset.

The good news is that you probably already know how to use this technique—we were all experts at this game when we were children! Nevertheless, here's a more systematic approach for using alter egos to bootstrap yourself to higher levels of mastery in your own practice.

Step 1: Identify the alter ego's essence

When embarking on your journey to practice a new skill, consider adopting the alter ego strategy by creating two contrasting personas. On one side, there's your familiar self, the comfort zone dweller and the self-doubter. This version holds you back, plays it safe, and cares too much about others' opinions. On the other side, you have your heroic self, the epitome of your best qualities, and the fearless one. This self lives in the moment, exudes confidence in abilities, and fearlessly takes on challenges.

The big caveat here, however, is not to think that the "old self" is a shameful baddie who is, unfortunately, the *real* you, while the heroic self is nice but "fake." The truth is, you possess qualities from both of these selves—right now you possess heroic traits, and they are already within you, just waiting to be developed and focused on. There's a reason so many kids' stories end up with the hero discovering that they "had it in them all along"—the alter ego is not fake at all, but just a kind of crutch you use until you can convince yourself that you were already that person.

Think of the old self as a role you could potentially choose to play as well. That's a mask you put on just as surely as you put on the hero's mask. The only difference is that to play that role, you consciously limit yourself and play small, whereas when you wear the hero mask, you don't hold back.

To start creating your alter ego, you need to think of the task ahead of you. For Natalie, it was doing a full standup routine without having a nervous breakdown. She analyzed that into a series of different tasks and then asked about the kind of person who would be able to do those tasks with ease. The later ego works best for the more mental skills and emotions that accompany the actual physical tasks you need to perform, for example:

- Calming your nerves (before a speech)
- Staying fully in the moment (singing opera)
- Being supremely focused (playing chess)
- Being resilient, i.e., not "spooked" by anything (martial arts)

- Being competitive, aggressive, in "attack mode" (horse riding, racing sports)
- Being quick and flowing effortlessly (delivering a lecture)
- Being confident (making a sales pitch)
- Staying limber and adaptable (dancing, painting)

You get the idea! Another way to identify the mental state you wish to emulate is to work backward: Look at where you currently are and invert it. For example, if you feel stiff and uncomfortable, zoom in on the state of mind of naturalness and ease. Another fun way to find the essence of your later ego is to ask yourself: if I could be a superhero right now, what superpower would most help me in my current practice?

Your alter ego may be based on just one main feeling, or it could be a blend of more than one, depending on your needs. Don't be afraid to create a few different alter egos for different situations or skills.

Step 2: Be Creative

Unleash the magic of this process by tapping into your imagination—a potent tool that is always at our disposal. Personalizing your alter ego with creativity and playfulness enhances your ability to really identify with it—and achieve consistent peak performance. What's their name? What do they look like? What's their "calling card"? Do they have any catchphrases or mottos? Are they from another planet? Are they maybe an animal— even a mythical animal? If they could talk to you, what might they say?

Have fun with this. While it might feel a little silly at first, give it a try—because it works! The only objective here is to create a unique identity that resonates with *you*. You never have to share this alter ego with anyone else, and it doesn't have to look like anyone else's either, so don't worry about being unconventional.

Your alter ego can be a blend of people you know in real life, role models, celebrities, or just a slightly improved version of yourself. If you like, incorporate mythical or religious elements, use imagery from art or media, and imbue your character with plenty of symbolism that will help you better connect to them. Natalie's alter ego Naomi is a seven-foot-tall redhead who is actually part fox and has the dress sense and hairdo of her favorite golden-era Hollywood actress, Lauren Bacall.

Your alter ego may be based on the Greek god of the sea, Poseidon, and you bring out his persona when you're doing the swimming portion of a triathlon. You tap into powerful feelings of commanding not just the sea, but your own regal self as you push yourself through the punishing water. Or maybe your alter ego is a smaller one: Whenever you go into the kitchen, you temporarily imagine yourself as a wise old Italian *nonna*. The tomato sauce tastes too sharp. What would *she* do if she were here in the kitchen with you now? (In an Italian accent, you tell yourself, "I'll just add a little sugar, no big deal . . .")

Alter egos can be especially useful if you're trying to learn another language. That's because language is closely connected to the place and culture that it sprang from. It's why we associate an upper-class British accent with sophistication and a certain uptightness, why we see French as sexy and libertine, and why we associate someone with an accent we can't identify as mysterious and exotic.

If you're learning a new language, you can deliberately give your alter ego a culture-bound identity. In other words, if you're learning French, you may actually learn faster if you create a French version of yourself and pretend to be them. You may create a vivid image of the French self in your mind (don't worry if you lean heavily into embarrassing or inaccurate stereotypes—it doesn't matter!).

You give this person a French name, dress them in French clothes, gives them French mannerisms, and make them talk about French things. People who are naturally good at picking up languages tend to do this unconsciously. They end up acquiring not just a new language but an entirely new way of being in the world.

Think carefully about how this principle may apply to your chosen field of mastery. If you're studying medicine, how can you embody the persona of an ideal physician? How does an accomplished doctor look, sound, and move? Or if you want to be an established and respected entrepreneur, ask yourself, how does such a person communicate? What is their lifestyle like, and how do they interact with others? What do they eat for breakfast?! Questions like these may seem silly, but the more psychological scaffolding you can identify for the state of mind you're aspiring to, the easier it will be to move yourself from where you are to where (or who!) you want to be.

Summary:

- The paradox of expertise is that when we know, we are immediately in a smaller, more limited frame of mind. To embrace humility and curiosity, cultivate a "beginner's mind." Build receptivity, curiosity, ambiguity, and playfulness, and be willing to say you don't know.

- Let go of assumptions and preconceptions, and deliberately seek out counterevidence for the things you believe to be true. With a growth mindset, you can reframe knowledge and skill as something malleable. Finally, invite awe and wonder into your life and immerse yourself in the unknown.

- There are two types of motivation: "Away-from" motivation involves avoiding something undesirable, while "toward" motivation revolves around striving toward a goal. We are all different and motivated by different things, our preferences themselves changing over time. Running away from something works, but it fundamentally contradicts the way that natural talents practice. Instead, frame your goals in positive terms, strike a balance between toward and away-from motivation, and work on interim goals/baby steps.

- Practice doesn't make perfect; perfect practice makes perfect. Don't worry about the quantity of practice you do, but its quality. Friedman recommends actively reflecting on your progress, monitoring your performance, keeping track of your goals, and continually adjusting your strategy as you go.

- Likewise, continually challenge yourself; don't keep rehearsing at the same level, but constantly push up against your current skill and comfort level. "Practice" can include mental rehearsal. Carefully conjure up the time, place, sensory details, and nuances of a scene you're rehearsing in your imagination.

- Finally, improve your performance by creating an alter ego to bridge the gap between your current ability and your aspired level of competence. Identify the character's essence, create a persona, then tap into your imagination to fuse with that role.

Part 3: You Need Flexibility

Change Things Up

Meet Daniel. He's the kind of guy who would have loved the story about Milo that we looked at earlier. More than anything in the world, Daniel relishes the feeling of physical mastery—he loves feeling strong, resilient, and capable. He loves the sensation of staring down a challenge and conquering it with nothing more than his bare hands, so to speak. And so for a few months now, he's been building his strength at the gym day by day and working on his self-discipline and confidence in the process.

He has the routine all lined up: He works out hard six days out of seven and rests on Fridays, and each day is devoted to a particular compound lift, which he trains to failure as often as he can. He's getting especially good at squats and is well on his way to being able to squat twice his body weight—a goal he never thought he'd achieve. Basically, Daniel is strong.

One day, his little sister challenges him to come to her ballet class—it'll be fun, she tells him. Daniel agrees reluctantly but guesses there could be . . . certain upsides. Within just fifteen minutes of the warmup exercises, however, Daniel politely excuses himself, red-faced and gasping for breath, as he tries to conceal the fact that his thigh muscles are on fire and he's close to falling over and never getting up again. He looks on as the class continues breezily moving through their *developpés* and *rond de jambes*.

He doesn't understand it—isn't he *strong*? What happened?

The issue here is that Daniel isn't really strong; it's more accurate to say he's good at doing the thing he keeps training himself to do: go to the gym, adopt a particular stance, position a standardized bar across a particular point on his shoulders, then move through a very specific sequence of motions, maintaining the very same form every time, then putting the bar down again, then going home again. Daniel is extremely good at this, along with the few other lifts he's mastered. But his mistake is to focus so exclusively on this small set of tasks that he's allowed himself to think that this is identical to "building strength."

When he attends the ballet class (a thing he assumed he'd do with ease), he is suddenly attempting something completely novel. He has to move his body in unfamiliar ways, using different muscles in different ways, to achieve control and poise in a manner he had never before thought to develop. And, despite having muscly legs like two thick tree stumps, he can't do it.

Researchers at Johns Hopkins have found that most people tend to focus on repetitive practice when trying to master a skill, such as endlessly shooting hoops from the same spot on the court or going through the same list of vocabulary words over and over again. They may create a false sense of their own competence . . . that is, until they enter an unfamiliar situation. Perhaps one day they encounter a basketball net that's not the usual height or size, or they have to talk on the spot to a native speaker without knowing what the conversation is going to be about. And they freeze. Suddenly, all that mastery seems to fly out the window!

Researchers suggest that practicing *a slightly modified version* of the task you want to master can lead to faster and more effective learning. By varying your practice, you can learn and improve more efficiently compared to just repeating the exact same thing multiple times in a row. The study explored the idea of reconsolidation, which is when existing memories are retrieved and then strengthened and modified with new knowledge. Lead researcher Pablo A. Celnik at the Johns Hopkins University School of Medicine explained that,

> "What we found is if you practice a slightly modified version of a task you want to master, you actually learn more and faster than if you just keep practicing the exact same thing multiple times in a row [...] Our results are important because little was known before about how reconsolidation works in relation to motor skill development. This shows how simple manipulations during training can lead to more rapid and larger motor skill gains because of reconsolidation [. . .] The goal is to develop novel behavioral interventions and training schedules that give people more improvement for the same amount of practice time."

Participants in a control group who didn't practice a modified version of a task actually performed twenty-five percent worse than participants who did switch up their practice. Luckily for Daniel, the researchers emphasize that it's only *minor* adjustments that are needed to get this improvement. So, Daniel might find that his weight training program is improved by just slightly changing the way he does his ordinary lifts. This might mean using bars of different thicknesses, practicing with and without gloves, working with and without chalk, training sometimes inside and sometimes outside, wearing different shoes or workout gear, or even attempting slight variations on form. This helps him improve faster and get more done when it comes to these specific exercises.

But what about Daniel's main goal—to be strong? If Daniel can find ways to incorporate other completely different kinds of training into his routine, he may find that he achieves this broader goal far more quickly. For example he could incorporate more flexibility and isometric exercises and work on his cardiovascular fitness. He could start including freeform exercises that challenge his body in a more holistic way, such as rock climbing, coasteering, martial arts, obstacle courses, calisthenics, or even parkour. By being challenged and developed in all these different ways, his strength is more comprehensive and robust than the "linear" strength he'd develop in the gym alone.

Let's explore another example to get a good idea of how to apply this principle—both to improve the immediate task at hand and also to improve more general capacities. We'll consider the example of preparing to deliver a specific speech on a set date.

Step 1: Rehearse the basic skill

Naturally, you need to start somewhere, so get back to basics and figure out the main skills you need to perform the specific tasks you're practicing. In this example, this may mean running through your speech once, in full, under exactly the same conditions as you expect to deliver it for real. You might not be able to get to the exact location, but let's say you're able to find a big hall that's roughly the same size, with a podium and setup not unlike the one you'll face on the big day. Your first practice is just to go through the speech in this way a few times without making too many mistakes and without getting too nervous.

Step 2: Wait and consolidate

Researchers believed that the best results came from allowing for a minimum of six hours between practice session variations. In this example, that should be pretty easy. You give it a rest and stop practicing for the day and plan to return the same time the next day to do your next practice session.

Step 3: Modify your practice session

Time to mix it up. The next day, you try a few different approaches, such as speaking slightly faster or slower, breaking the presentation into smaller parts, or practicing under different conditions. Maybe you experiment with different gestures and tone of voice, slightly switch the order of some of your slides, or position yourself differently on the podium.

Step 4: Modify and refine

Keep going! Don't stop after just one round of variations. Keep practicing with different tweaks and adjustments. Each time you practice, focus on refining specific aspects of your speaking, such as vocal variety, body language, or storytelling techniques. You want to keep the variation slight enough that it's still essentially the same speech, but you're doing what Daniel did when he slightly changed the type of bar he used or switched up his gym shoes. You're just exploring that narrow little zone around the skill you're developing.

Step 5: Don't forget to "cross train"

What else might help you indirectly strengthen the skills you're trying to master? Only you can answer this question, but in our example we can imagine that things like learning breath control, relaxation and mindfulness exercises, practice with elocution and enunciation, or simply methods for boosting confidence. Here's where you can get creative with mental rehearsal, too.

By the time you've run through the above process a few times, you really will feel like you know your speech inside and out and that you can tackle it even if it should suddenly throw you a curve ball on the day. Because you've not only practiced the skill itself but also trained a degree of flexibility, you are more resilient and more creative.

On the day, you get up to the podium to make your speech, and you're struck by the fact that it feels like this is the hundredth time you're doing it—you're not nervous at all. You can deliver that speech with your eyes closed. On the way up to the podium, however, you suddenly trip on a cable that isn't ordinarily there, but is on this occasion because of the lighting that's been set up for the event. You stumble and, without thinking about it, make a quick joke that has people roaring with laughter. None of it was planned, but because you're so relaxed, you quickly recover and make the best of it. You get to the podium, smile, and make your speech.

On the spur of the moment, you decide to subtly change the first part just based on the mood you're in and your intuition for what you think people might like. The audience loves it. You've taken a step toward not just being a great orator, but someone who can calmly and confidently speak even without notes or prompts. Because of the way you trained in flexibility, you are not thrown by the unexpected and actually end up overshooting and learning more than you even set out to.

Flexibility is not just what you do, but how you do it. It's a mindset. As you practice with subtle variations, you are also teaching yourself to be limber and adaptable. You are simultaneously teaching yourself a kind of resilience and aliveness to the moment.

When we practice, we can sometimes set up artificial scenarios and ultra-safe setups that don't really reflect the real world. But when you deliberately switch up what you're doing, you develop a kind of mental suppleness that makes you stronger in the face of the unknown, rather than more vulnerable. Throw in a wild card now and then, try something new (like your little sister's ballet class), and be willing to think on your feet. At the same time, don't get too confident training a very narrow range of skills—keep reminding yourself of what that skill looks like *in vivo.*

Know When to Take a Break

Let's revisit an important point from the previous section—the value of taking a rest. Though it may seem paradoxical at first, sometimes the best way to *do* something is not to do it at all.

Imagine that you're working your way through endless chemistry questions in an attempt to practice for the exam you have coming up in a few weeks. Time is short and you're doing your best to cram. You wake up early, seal yourself in your study, and get stuck into paper after paper, answering tricky practice questions so that when you're facing the real exam paper, you'll know exactly what to do. By 4 p.m. that afternoon, your brain is mush, but you keep going. You encounter an especially challenging glitch that you just can't seem to work out. The problem is you keep getting a particular kind of question wrong, but you don't know why. It's driving you mad!

Finally you give up and concede defeat, and head to bed at midnight, exhausted.

In the morning you wake up and go to your study again for round two. This time you look at the questions that stumped you yesterday and think to yourself, "Oh, I get it now," and you solve it.

Has something like this ever happened to you? It turns out, you might not even need a long sleep overnight to get similar "aha" moments. We all sometimes make the mistake of thinking that it's *only* active and conscious effort that yields results. It's what makes us stay up till midnight hacking away at a problem. But rest is vitally important—the big rests *and* the small ones.

A study conducted by researchers at the National Institutes of Health (NIH) reveals the critical role that resting plays in the process of learning new skills. Contrary to the common belief of continuous practice, the study found that taking short breaks during learning may be just as crucial as practice itself. The research involved recording the brainwaves of healthy volunteers as they practiced typing numbers with their left hands, followed by short breaks.

Surprisingly, the volunteers' **performance improved primarily during the rest periods, with brainwaves indicating memory consolidation happening during those breaks**. The changes in brainwaves, specifically in the right hemispheres and neural networks associated with movement planning, correlated with the improvements seen during the rests. This is an important point—the learning itself was happening *outside* of the practice session, not during.

According to study lead Leonardo G. Cohen, senior investigator at NIH's National Institute of Neurological Disorders and Stroke, "Everyone thinks you need to 'practice, practice, practice' when learning something new. Instead, we found that resting, early and often, may be just as critical to learning as practice."

Long periods of rest, such as sleeping overnight, are extremely valuable, but the researchers wanted to challenge the idea that this was the only way to consolidate learning. When the team analyzed their data, not only did they discover that improvements were made in rest periods, but they also discovered that **the gains made during the shorter "waking" rest periods between practice sessions were greater than the gains made between daily sessions**, i.e., after the participants returned the next day and did the tasks again after a night's sleep. That means that smaller rest periods were more powerful than longer periods of sleep.

During a rest period, the brain is consolidating everything it has learned during the more active phase of practice—and this is observable in the changes of brainwaves patterning in the brain. Now, the research team was especially interested in using their findings to help people who've experienced stroke to rehabilitate and relearn the skills they lost. While they have not tested whether their conclusions would work for ordinary people who want to better master their chosen skill, it's worth paying attention to how you schedule your own break time when you practice.

Instead of "practice, practice, practice," it may be more effective to "practice, rest, practice, rest." It may be that taking even micro-breaks of around ten seconds during your practice can help your brain properly absorb what it's learned. After every repetition you make, pause a little; during that moment it will be as though your brain quickly replays a compressed memory of what you've just experienced. The researchers discovered that the brain literally goes over a version of what you've just practiced, only about twenty times faster—taking just a few seconds. Interestingly, they also found that the first few practice sessions tended to be the most critical for this process.

If you just barge ahead without taking breaks of any size, you never give yourself that chance to consolidate and may find that you tend to forget huge chunks of what you already covered. You may even notice that after a long, hard study session, you seemingly can only remember the last few minutes of it, for example. That's because the more separate instances of rest, the more effectively you learn. If you rest only once, you effectively consolidate only once—and it doesn't matter how long that rest was.

Thinking of rest in this way reframes a break as a hidden "rep" where you are actively giving the idea time to sink in. It's like gradually pouring water into a potted plant. You pour some, wait for it to soak in, then pour a little more. This "spacing effect" not only feels more comfortable, but will help you learn more quickly in less time, without you needing to burn yourself out.

There's value in medium rest periods, too. According to *Time* magazine, the perfect break is having a seventeen-minute break after fifty-two minutes of practice/work. Built into this, however, can be many dozens of smaller ten-second breaks after each new chunk of information or repetition is encountered. Then, on the biggest scale, you have longer periods of deeper rest when you sleep each day.

How to Rest

It may seem strange to have a "how to" when it comes to rest, but many of us genuinely get it wrong. Perhaps because we're so used to overvaluing the active, deliberate portion of our practice that we forget how to literally stop and do nothing. We may, for example, ask questions like "What's the most effective way to rest?" as though we can apply the same measure of productivity to what our brain does automatically and passively.

The only "rule" of resting is that you *have to genuinely rest*. That means do nothing. Don't think about what you're going to do next or what you have already done. Don't consciously try to carry on working in your head. During the work period, give your tasks your full attention and make progress. Then completely disengage from work during the break, allowing your brain to rest and refresh.

There is a caveat to the do-nothing rule, however, and that is that you can also rest by immersing yourself in a completely different task. For example, if you've been using your brain all morning and you need a break, don't "rest" by reading if that book is fiction and something you do just for fun. This will be somewhat relaxing, but it won't be a complete rest because your brain is still working. Instead, you might go outdoors for a walk or run and just let your mind loosen and empty, even though your body might suddenly be very active.

In the same way, many students have accidentally discovered that even if they sacrifice a few hours of study and socialize into the night instead, they are mysteriously more refreshed the next morning than if they had studied and gone to bed early. That's because even though they were physically awake and socializing till late, they were still giving their academic mind the chance to completely switch off and recharge. It goes the other way, too. If you've been training hard all day and your muscles are tired and sore, vegging out on the sofa with a challenging crossword may still register as a break—from your body's point of view, anyway!

What to Do about Procrastination

To summarize briefly, in order to practice effectively, you need

1. a strategic roadmap,
2. the right mindset to keep yourself chipping away at that roadmap, and

3. enough flexibility to survive and adapt when things don't go to plan.

Mixing things up, taking a break, and regularly stepping back to assess and adjust are just as important as putting your head down and doing the work. The real skill of flexibility, then, is about *discernment*—the ability to know when to rest, when to push, when to zoom in to the details, when to step back and give things a re-think, when to try harder, when to try smarter.

In *The Practicing Mind*, author Thomas M. Sterner digs into these questions and more. It would seem that there are really **two** things you're learning every time you commit to mastering a new skill: the competence of the skill itself and the mental competence required for you to do what it takes to learn that skill. It wouldn't be an exaggeration to say that most of us fail at our goals not because we lack the skill to accomplish the task itself, but because we blunder with the second part, the mental competency holding it all together.

According to Sterner, a massive impediment is not a lack of aptitude, intelligence, or even passion, but **too much anxiety**. Let's look at some of the major ways he believes we end up succumbing to anxiety and sabotaging ourselves.

Unrealistic Expectations

Let's say you had the goal to learn how to use a certain piece of design software, and you achieved that goal. Then you headed onto Instagram and saw a twenty-one-year-old who's not only mastered that program but several others, and they've produced works that blow you away—in a bad way. You think, "Well, what's the point? I'll never get there. This is too hard."

But this is an error. No matter what you do, there will always be someone further along than you. Really, read that sentence again— even the enviously talented twenty-one-year-old looks at their role models and feels intimidated. So what? It's normal to feel that sense of frustration that comes with having a shifting goalpost, but *don't allow it to determine what you do*. In other words, don't let the perfect be the enemy of the good.

This goes beyond comparisons on social media or the nonsense fed to us by the media and advertising. It speaks directly to a pre-existing human tendency to entertain ideals of perfection that are far beyond what is reasonable to expect of ourselves (or anyone). Holding this shifting horizon in our mind's eye, we then can't help but devalue our achievements, whatever they are. Compared against perfection, nothing ever will be enough, and so the paradox of these high standards is that we tend to do less toward our goals, not more.

Be on guard: Watch out for immediately shifting your goal the second you've achieved it. It's great to look ahead at an inspiring and aspirational vision of the future. But temper this with an acknowledgment of how far you've advanced from where you started. Don't compete with others; instead tap into your own values and use those as a yardstick for yourself. This will reduce your anxiety and increase what matters—deliberate practice toward your goals.

Process, Not Outcome

A related problem is to focus too much on the future and not enough on the only place where you have real control and can take useful action: the present.

Are you a procrastinator? There's a good chance you stall because you're too good at looking at the bigger picture, the end result, and the total project lying before you. You're not so good at realizing that this big intimidating project doesn't have to be done all at once—all you need to concern yourself with is the very next step in the sequence.

It is the perception itself that is intimidating you, not the size of the task. If you think about running a marathon, you are keenly aware that it takes a whopping forty thousand steps. But this conceals the reality of running a marathon—you literally can only do one step at a time. The idea of the forty thousand number stresses you out; the idea of the single step doesn't. It would be so much easier to run a marathon, in fact, if you didn't even call it a marathon. Just call it "taking a single step" but done forty thousand times.

Focusing too much on the end goal can be discouraging because we remind ourselves of how far away it is. We see the distance between where we are and where we "should" be, and that feels like a problem. In fact, the real issue is when we take the perspective that the distance from the goal is somehow an indicator of our progress, or even perhaps an indicator of competence and worth as people. But being at the start of the marathon isn't fundamentally a worse place to be than in the middle or at the end.

Be on guard: Set yourself a good, clear goal that makes sense to you, and then forget about it. Your practice happens in the here and now, today, in this moment. Don't make the final step of that marathon mean more than all the other steps—it doesn't. Your goal is to figure out how to do your next step. That's all. Do this and there will be a moment when you can look back and notice the thousands of steps you've taken. But that moment will take care of itself and come when it comes, without you needing to worry about it.

Do, Observe, Correct

Sterner suggests a three-step method for getting yourself out of productivity slumps caused by anxiety or overwhelm. At its heart, it's about flexibility and discernment: You learn to be aware, monitor yourself, and then make intelligent decisions about how to adjust and adapt. This is a fundamentally *active* approach and continually acknowledges the fact that the only person in charge of your development is YOU.

To simplify, the method allows you to notice when you are straying away from your practice roadmap, to observe the exact behavior that's going on, and then to make whatever correction is required for you to keep going effectively. What you *don't* do is remain ignorant of why you're losing productivity, fail to identify the cause of it, or miss an opportunity to fine-tune your approach.

Now, this may all seem a little abstract and vague, so let's take a look at a concrete example. We'll consider what doesn't work—

and what Sterner suggests is a better approach.

Jo is a talented and passionate ceramic artist and has been working on her own unique glazing technique that produces strikingly beautiful results. A local craft collective wants her to set up a section in their venue so that she can showcase some of her pieces, but that means she'll have to work quickly to create some brilliant new pieces that really show off her skills. She agrees to produce twenty pieces in the next month and is originally excited. Then, procrastination hits.

Her production grinds to a halt, and she can't seem to peel herself off the couch and get into the studio. Her friends are mystified—Jo has easily produced thirty or forty pieces a month for years, and now is suddenly intimidated by the prospect of doing half of that. Jo has practiced her art and craft very diligently, taught herself everything, and has been super disciplined. More than anything, she wants to take the next step and start working with bigger businesses to sell her work and get more visibility. In other words, at this point in her "practice," Jo lacks neither a motivating reason nor the necessary skill. She has supportive friends and an opportunity staring her in the face. And she still procrastinates.

Here's the *wrong* way Jo could go about things: She could conclude that the problem is that she is "lazy" and "has an issue with procrastination." She could start to wonder if she's even cut out for this career she's chosen for herself, and whether she ever had any real talent to begin with. What's wrong with her to waste such a great opportunity? Eventually she feels so ashamed and demoralized, she calls the venue and tells them to just cancel the whole thing and give her place to someone else.

Here's a better way she could approach the problem:

First, she notices what she is actually doing. Yes, procrastination is something you DO! Jo sets aside any feelings of self-criticism and judgment and just looks at the situation for what it is. She notices that she sets an intention to go into the studio, then quickly thinks to herself, "This is your one chance, Jo, so you better not blow it. They want those twenty pieces in just a few weeks, so there's no time to mess around."

She notices then that she sits down, gets to work, applies the glaze too thin, and then it crystallizes and goes milky, marring the finish. "It's ruined," she thinks. She's so upset she takes a little break. The little break turns into a marathon social media scrolling session, and before she knows it, she's procrastinating for days.

Can you see why?

- **Unrealistic expectations**: Jo has overemphasized the importance of this task so much that she will only accept one hundred percent perfection. She tells herself, "It has to be perfect or else." Her first attempt *isn't* perfect, so she freaks out and quits. She seems to forget that her first attempt often does turn out a little milky, and it's usually no big deal . . .
- **Overfocus on outcome**: As prolific as Jo is, she never produces twenty pieces in just one day. And yet, when she steps into that studio, she's assigning herself this very task: Produce twenty pieces, and they'd better be perfect, and do it *now*.

This is the DO and the OBSERVE part of the formula. Now comes the part where Jo can CORRECT.

When people say that they have a problem with procrastination, they are really misdiagnosing the situation. Their problem is in their *thoughts* about their situation. Jo would be making a mistake if she started to second guess her talent or her love for ceramics. It would be a big mistake to conclude that "This is too hard. I'm just not disciplined or talented enough to do it." These things are not the problem. Her real issue is not the nature of the task ahead of her, but the way she's thinking about it.

This is what she needs to correct—her thinking.

Much advice out there on beating procrastination makes the mistake of suggesting ways to modify the task. This can help, but only because it indirectly changes the thinking, perception, and appraisal. And that's what matters.

For Jo, what needs to change is the thinking that causes her overwhelming anxiety. That means the unrealistic expectations, the unattainable goals, and the overfocus on the outcome at the expense of just working with the process. Jo gets real with herself and sits down to work through this *do*, *observe*, *correct* process.

She decides to reframe the way she's thinking about things. She tells herself, "Look, Jo, this is a lucky opportunity, and it will be great to get the best out of it. But it's not the only chance you'll ever get, and even if it doesn't go to plan, it won't be the end of the world. The stakes may feel high, but you're really just doing what you already know how to do. Your goal for tomorrow is just to dial things back and focus on producing *one piece*. Take your time. Think carefully about that glazing issue and just focus on getting that right, for just that one piece. Never mind about the rest of it for now." This is the key to breaking her inertia. She goes into the studio, starts up again, and soon she has found her old momentum and is working happily.

In your own life, you might find this approach useful to draw on when you're in the middle of a crisis. Perhaps you've lost your mojo, you're feeling a bit lost, or you're suddenly facing procrastination like Jo. Consciously decide not to judge yourself or avoid the situation. Instead, take a step back, be as neutral and objective as you can, and just notice what you're doing and what you can do better.

If we're honest, most of us get in our own way when it comes to developing mastery and truly developing. We allow doubt and self-judgment and fear to derail us, even though we possess all the skills and capacities to achieve success. Here are a few more tips if you find yourself hitting a wall:

Give yourself permission to play. When we are afraid of how we're performing, we freeze up and become rigid. Instead, see what happens when you actively give yourself the space and freedom to play, mess around, and just explore. Take the performance element out completely and just get moving again. Many writers destroy their writer's block by regularly giving themselves permission to write poorly.

Give yourself permission to think small. You sit down to practice, and you realize it's not much fun. You remember that you need to practice to reach the Big Goal. You realize just how far away from it you are. You get discouraged and disappointed. It's pretty tiring to feel that way, so you seek some kind of relief to make yourself feel better. You procrastinate. The next time you sit down to practice, the Big Goal is just as important and scary and intimidating as always, but now there's an extra dose of shame at avoiding it. This feels bad, too. So you need relief. And round and round you go.

One way to break this cycle—think smaller. Stop reminding yourself of the Big Goal.

Maintain your focus. The process isn't a one-and-done affair. For example, Jo gets to work making ceramics again, but she is vigilant and watches what she does and notices when her productivity and motivation start dropping.

The second they do, she pauses and observes and makes the necessary corrections. The finer and more frequent the adjustments she makes, the more effective she is overall. She no longer gets super trapped in procrastination because she learns how to nip it in the bud well before it gets out of hand.

Don't Avoid Failure, Analyze It

How do you respond to failure?

Try to think right now about the last time you messed up and what it really felt like.

Maybe you made a silly but embarrassing typo in an important document you prepared for a higher-up. Maybe you completely forgot a significant date or made a mess of a DIY project you felt sure you'd manage. Big or small, you can probably recall that rush of panic and fear once you realize what's happened, and the immediate feeling of "Oh crap, this is *bad*!"

Making mistakes is human, but in the middle of one, we can feel so uniquely stupid and incompetent, like we are the only ones in the universe to get things wrong sometimes. The way our world is set up, mistakes can feel more dangerous and unacceptable than they really are, and we can tell ourselves all sorts of stories about how a mistake means more than it really does—for example, that we're bad people, we do things badly, and we always will. We can even try to inflict the misery of failure and mistakes on other people, resorting to blaming them, the task itself, or just the whole world and how unfair and stupid it is.

Failure, however, is guaranteed. It *will* happen, and if it's happened once, it will happen again.

What is not set in stone is our response to it. How we perceive, explain, and make sense of failure is extremely variable and very much under our control. When we feel ashamed and uncomfortable about making a mistake, there's typically one thing we do: avoid. We run away from the situation and try to escape that awful feeling. We blame ourselves or others ("Who's fault is this?"—well, nobody's . . .), or we try to cover it all up and move on as quickly as possible.

If we approach failure with a different attitude, however, we don't avoid but *approach*. We turn toward our failure and say to it, "Oh, hi, you're interesting. What can you teach me?" The irony is that you can only really make use of failure if you're willing to embrace it—and that means not thinking of it in terms of "failure" at all, but rather just something that happens on the way to mastery. In fact, a mistake is not even a failure. It's just a mistake. It doesn't mean anything unless you make it mean something. What happens next is up to you.

Josh is a brilliant gymnast and is quickly earning a reputation for his precision, artistry, and energetic performance. He's just fifteen but nobody doubts that his path is going to lead him straight to Olympic stardom. He spends his life in the gym, and one day he is working on his nemesis—the parallel bars. Josh is agile, but his wrist strength has never been his forte, and he's having to work on his coordination.

From a toe-on entry, he transitions to a van Leeuwen half twist, but then fails to bring his left arm to the bar quickly enough, so he repeatedly knocks his knuckles and ends up rushing to the next move. His trainer points it out, but Josh repeats the same mistake, and then repeats it a third time. He's starting to feel humiliated, and his knuckles really hurt. His trainer tells him to relax and slow down. But Josh's humiliation makes him do the opposite—speed up. It's as though in trying to just get that portion of the move over and done with, he is caught by it even more. Eventually, in frustration, he comes off the bars, yells at his trainer (that's another mistake), and storms out.

Josh's problem is not that he's bad at gymnastics, or even bad at the parallel bars. In fact, he's better than the vast majority of human beings. His "mistake" is really just a single area where he has yet to gain mastery. That's all. But with the wrong mindset, it starts to look like a lot more than this. And so Josh actually prevents himself from learning. He gets stuck.

Eventually Josh cools down and comes back into the gym. His trainer, who knows a thing or two about failure, tells him to get back on the bars. Josh agrees but says he won't bother with the van Leeuwen half twist today—he's over it. The trainer smiles and shakes his head. He tells Josh that on the contrary, for the rest of the day, that's the *only* thing they're going to bother with. He knows that until you can calmly face mistakes, you cannot learn from them.

Try to recall again the last time you made a mistake. Did you avoid it or approach it? Did you judge yourself, or did you become curious about how you could use the experience?

Tip 1: Own it

Your knee-jerk reaction may be to blame something or somebody else. Resist this urge and take full responsibility for your mistakes as early as you can. It's not the bar's fault, it's not the trainer's fault, and it's not the fault of the gym air conditioning or the fact that it's

Tuesday or because you woke up late this morning because your alarm malfunctioned.

That said, don't blame yourself, either. Instead, take responsibility (that's not the same as blaming). If you are the one who made it happen, then it means you are the one who can make something else happen. Blame others and you just keep yourself passive and unable to improve.

Just look at the mistake and acknowledge it was something you did. No, it's something you are, but it is something you did. Look at it as clearly and honestly as you can. "I'm not leaving the first bar with enough momentum because I'm rushing, and that means I don't have the time to get my left hand in the right position. That's something I'm doing." (Note: "I messed up because I'm a big stupid idiot face" is the kind of language you want to avoid!).

Tip 2: Reframe

How you talk about your mistake influences how you feel about it, and that changes how you might act moving forward. If you interpret your failure as an opportunity, you feel motivated to take that opportunity and get what you can from the experience. You take action. If you interpret the mistake as par for the course and no big deal, you feel pretty calm and neutral about it, and you simply carry on with your practice.

There are lots of different ways to frame your experience. There is no "right" and "wrong"—but some ways of framing will result in you feeling empowered and motivated, and therefore taking useful action, while others will paralyze you and make you feel like garbage. You make the choice, and you make that choice by deciding how you'll appraise your mistake.

Often, our beliefs and thoughts about things run through our mind so quickly that we don't get a chance to really notice them. For Josh, he might need to reframe things and remind himself that even though he's brilliant, he's not perfect . . . and he doesn't need to be. Making mistakes is normal and nothing to feel ashamed about. How do *you* think about failure, and how do those beliefs influence how you feel and how you practice?

Is a mistake something embarrassing to conceal from others, or just no big deal?
Does a mistake tell you about your value as a person, or just give you information about your stage of development?

Is a mistake an opportunity or a loss of opportunity?
Is a mistake a sign that you're doing things wrong, or proof that you're doing exactly what you should be?

Tip 3: Mine for data

When you first realized the big typo you made in the document, your only thought was "Oh crap, this is bad!"

But what kind of bad? Why is it bad? Exactly how is it bad? Is it entirely bad, or is just a portion of it bad?

If you can sit with your discomfort for a little while, you can start to analyze your mistake and say something more about it than "It's wrong, it's wrong, it's wrong."

Become curious about the nature of the mistake and what it's telling you to do better next time. What were you attempting to do? Why did you not manage to do it? At precisely what point did things go wrong? Why?

Let these questions start shaping a lesson in your mind. If X didn't work last time, try Y now. If you made the mistake because you went too slow, then speed up the next time.

Once you've done the big postmortem, you can use that data to feed back into your practice. Whatever you do, don't just go back to your old routine and do the same thing again. Making a mistake can feel bad, but the best way to get over that bad feeling is actually to take action as soon as possible and do better.

In Josh's case, he sets to work with his trainer, breaking down the relevant moves into tiny components and drilling each one separately, going very slowly so they can identify the snag and remove it. Within half an hour, the problem is solved. What's more, Josh may have realized that losing his temper with his trainer was also something he should own and learn from—not to mention apologize for.

Learning and improving means change, and change can be hard. It takes a little humility because no human being ever moved from beginner to master without a few awkward phases in between. Try not to be afraid of seeking help, support, advice, and feedback. If you see someone else doing what you want to learn to do, don't get envious or feel bad about yourself, but be inspired instead. Ask for help and guidance and be prepared to listen and learn. Nothing will get you out of that awkward beginner phase faster!

Tip 4: Focus on flaws

Focus on your flaws, really? Yes. But do it in the right way.

Coyle explains how the most effective practice happens when people are intensely attuned to their mistakes and deficits, but all while holding a particular mindset. They are keenly aware of the differences between their actual skill level and the aspirational skill level, but they use awareness of this difference to motivate, not judge themselves.

You might not necessarily make an obvious "mistake" but rather notice that you're not quite doing a thing in an optimal way. It's important that you don't just make a note and move on. Rather, consciously stop, take a look at the imperfect action, and compare it against the ideal, then do whatever is necessary to get it closer to what it should be. The trick here is to do this entire process dispassionately and without judgment. Your current skill level is not wrong or bad. It's just what action looks like on the road to mastery. You are in process.

Here's a simplified explanation of how that process may play out:

- **Take action using your current knowledge.** Start practicing the skill you want to develop. If you're practicing filmmaking, for example, start with what you already know, which might be composing great steady shots.

- **Observe how things go and gather data by keeping a practice log**. You might keep a simple log, write down your practice observations, and then rate your skill improvement from one to ten. For example, keep a simple filmmaking journal or log where you reflect on your daily practice sessions. Write down how you felt during the process, your own skill rating, and any moments where you felt particularly inspired or motivated.

- **Note any mistakes and analyze what went wrong.** Identifying the source of fault enables you to address the issue effectively and focus on resolving the problem. Spotting mistakes effectively involves asking yourself three questions:

  1. **Is the cause internal or external?** Basically, is it your

fault or the fault of something or someone else?

For example, applying this to filmmaking: if you struggle with maintaining steady shots, it could be an internal issue related to your camera-handling skills, or an external factor like a faulty tripod. Be as honest and neutral as possible.

2. Is the cause constant, or does it change? A constant cause of error (like physics) can't be changed, but a variable cause of error (like lack of effort) can be changed.

Determine whether the cause of the error is constant or variable. If it's a constant cause, like the physical limitations of your equipment, you may need to work around it or find creative solutions. However, if the cause is variable, such as not putting enough effort into planning your shots, you have the opportunity to make changes and improve.

3 - Can the cause be controlled? What can you do about the source of the error?

Assess whether you have control over the cause of the error. If the cause is within your control, consider what actions you can take to address it. For instance, if you realize that poor lighting is affecting your shots, you can learn lighting techniques and invest in better equipment. However, if the cause is beyond your control, like unpredictable weather during outdoor shoots, you may need to adapt your plans accordingly. Acceptance is going to play a big role.

- **Use your mistake analysis to implement changes in your next practice routine.** Based on your assessment of the source of errors, plan a new practice session that focuses on fixing your mistakes. For instance, if you find out that your error is struggling with steady shooting, focus on camera handling or get a tripod for the next practice session.

Notice how in all the above steps, there is never any need to get defensive, avoidant, or upset about mistakes. There's also no point in noticing a mistake and proceeding to do the same thing over again. Be grateful for the mistakes you make—they're your teachers, if you'll listen to them.

Meta-Learning and the Bigger Picture

We've already covered in some detail the flexible, humble mindset you need to ride out failure and get the best of it. We've explored ways to take ownership for mistakes you make, reframe how you're thinking about it (i.e., it's an opportunity, not a threat), get curious about the data you can extract from the experience, and finally, rather than avoiding and escaping flaws, zooming in on them so you can get a really good idea of what you need to do better next time.

That's all well and good, but let's take things a step further. Consider the story of Emily. She's always been fascinated by the human body and how it works, and so it made perfect sense to her that she should study something to do with anatomy, exercise, or helping people with physical ailments. Emily soon devoted years of her life to training in the field, and accrued hours and hours of practical work where she examined, diagnosed, and treated all sorts of injuries, aches, and pains.

Emily has become extremely good at what she does and is a quick learner. She easily understands her mistakes, adjusts, and moves on from them. She has a solid work ethic and a good routine and has just the right kind of growth mindset that has consistently earned her a place at the top of every class she's taken.

So, what's the problem? Well, it's six years into Emily's journey as a physical therapist and she's just about to open her own practice. Everything is lined up and ready to go, and there's no reason to believe she cannot have a lucrative and successful practice. A few weeks before she's due to open her doors, she has a major meltdown as a terrifying new realization dawns on her: She doesn't even want to be a physical therapist.

Emily did *everything* right. She took the advice covered in this book and applied it completely, and then some. She learned to be the best physical therapist she could be. What she didn't do, however, was really stop to reflect on what she was learning, why, and what she intended to do with what she learned.

She didn't think too critically about the various pressures and demands on her that were motivating her decision to take this path, and she never gave herself the chance to fully explore options, to get creative with possibilities, or to shape her own learning experience. In other words, she was good at learning and acquiring skills, but not at stepping back and thinking about what those skills meant in her life, how they fit together, and what problems she intended to solve with them. Basically, she was no good at *meta-learning*.

David Kolb is a theorist interested in all the ways that people learn, big and small, and he proposes that people's overall learning styles are influenced by their life experiences, genetics, and the demands of the present. It's about so much more than simply what happens when you sit down at a desk to study or pick up an instrument and start playing. Rather, learning, growth, and mastery of new skills is always embedded in a bigger context and goes beyond its most superficial skills and tasks.

The Kolb learning cycle is a model of learning where learners move through a spiral of

1. immediate experience
2. reflection on that experience

3. abstractly conceptualizing the experience (by linking it with the past or, in general, "learning from the experience")
4. translating that learning into theories, actions, and experiments that apply what you know to the world

Kolb used this model to enhance self-directed study for his students at Stanford University, but we can use the framework to help us structure our own meta-learning in all areas of learning, not just academic subjects.

The model is flexible and can be applied at many different levels and for many different skills and tasks. Let's consider how the model might apply to the relatively simple task of learning to embroider. As you read, try to imagine how the model applies to Emily's story—and how it might explain where she went wrong with her career choice!

Immediate Experience

This is, broadly speaking, the moment we practice and engage with the nitty-gritty of learning something new. At this stage, the learner shows personal involvement with a concrete situation. The experience is at this point rather open-ended and free, and more about creative flow and immersion in the novelty of a new idea or concept.

For example, this may be the experience of delving into the fascinating world of embroidery, fiber art, and embellishment. Someone may discover a whole new world and find that it's not only interesting, but that they also seem to have a real knack for it. They pick up a needle and thread and start messing around with it, but quickly find they're addicted and wanting to learn more.

Reflection on that Experience

At this stage, learners pause, take a step back, and seek to understand the greater context of what they're learning, bringing a little objectivity to the picture. This is not about action; rather, it's about weighing up options, considering alternatives, and making meaning.

In our example, the person might stop for a moment and consider what they'd like to do next. They can see that embroidery has the potential to become a very expensive and time-consuming hobby. They have admired the work of brilliantly talented artists who create masterpieces, but also have seen that many people make wonderful intermediate projects that they use at home or gift to friends. So they start to ask themselves, just what would they like to do with this skill of embroidery, anyway? How much money and time do they have to blow on a new hobby? Do they intend for it to be a hobby, or would they like to make "art" embroidery or even sell pieces? What style do they most admire, and is this within the realm of possibility, given their skills and limitations?

Abstractly Conceptualizing the Experience

At this level, we link our learning experiences to the past or to other existing frameworks of knowledge so that we can start learning from them. At this level, you are striving to understand the essence behind the skill you're practicing. You may use ideas, logic, and theoretical models (a bit like Kolb's theory itself!) to start shaping your practice and help you understand what you're doing. By conceptualizing your learning in abstract terms, you can start to structure and plan your learning in a systematic way, and this in turn can help you solve problems and set goals.

What does all this look like when applied to embroidery?

Let's say the embroidery enthusiast eventually moves beyond just tinkering around with materials and starts to use a more deliberate approach. They decide that they're going to focus on the aspects of embroidery they love most—the intricacy and delicate geometric shapes of the works they most admire.

The person decides to focus exclusively on those techniques and aesthetics that emphasize these features (and ignores work that is about vibrancy, clothing, or flamboyant colors). They sign up for a course on the Japanese *Temari* technique—a folk art consisting of embellishing balls of different sizes with elaborate geometric designs worked in thread. The person in our example loves this form of embroidery not because of the embroidery itself but because of the essence behind the skill that they enjoy—the patience, diligence, and skill needed to closely approximate perfection.

Translating that Learning into Theories, Actions, and Experiments

The next stage is about moving into action again, but *actions that are inspired by the insights and reflections from the previous levels.* Here, the learner actively tries to experiment, try out new things, and test out theories, approaches, or novel ideas.

For our embroiderer, that may eventually mean moving on from patterns that others have written and branching out into creating and implementing their own designs. Perhaps, inspired by their love of intricacy and complexity, they challenge themselves to make extremely tiny *temari*, or use progressively finer and finer threads. In this way, they start to discover their own unique style and vision for the art form. However, reaching this stage is not possible unless the previous stages have been worked through.

You'll notice as well that the stages are laid out in a circle—they're not linear processes but stages followed in sequence over and over as you gain expertise and grow. In other words, since learning never really ends, your meta-learning shouldn't end either.

According to Kolb, people vary in their abilities and have stronger preferences for some parts of this cycle compared to others. A focus on each quadrant implies a kind of learning "style"; some people may be better at abstract conceptualization, for example, while others may spend more time naturally in a more concrete, experiencing mode.

Let's take a step back and try to understand Emily's predicament through this lens.

1. Immediate experience—Emily discovers she likes human anatomy and is good at it.
2. Reflection on that experience—uhh, Emily doesn't really do this.
3. Abstractly conceptualizing the experience—she doesn't do this either.
4. Translating that learning into theories, actions, and experiments—she definitely doesn't do this.

In fact, what happens in Emily's story is that, after having her immediate experience, she essentially stops her meta-learning and immerses herself in an external curriculum, conforming herself to its demands. She's great at the very first stage (concrete experience), but not the others. She gets on track to become a physical therapist and simply works to meet the demands of her course, one after another, in the prescribed way. She does not stop to reflect on her options and alternatives, and she certainly doesn't acknowledge the essence of what's behind her chosen task—i.e., what is it exactly about physical therapy that appeals to her?

Without an abstract conception of her study, she can't grasp that there are other ways to engage with what she finds interesting. She doesn't realize, then, that she can potentially take her study in other directions. With no chance to experiment, she never really learns what works and what doesn't when it comes to the study path itself. And so Emily finds herself in a place where many people find themselves when they are hard-working but lacking insight: in a great job that they don't really like.

Now, if your practice goal is not as big and serious as a career path, you may not need to use Kolb's theory in quite as much depth. Even with those tasks you don't believe to have a "bigger picture," it's worth regularly zooming out and becoming curious not just about how well you're learning, but where that learning fits into your overall life goals. Whether your practice area is something small (like an embroidery hobby) or much bigger (like your chosen career), take a moment to bolster your own meta-learning by asking the following questions:

Why exactly do you want to learn this task?

What is the essence or core behind this task that most appeals to you?

What other options or alternatives are there for accessing that essence?

If you've chosen a formal curriculum to follow, how well does that course serve your own needs and goals?

Can you adapt that curriculum or set your own path?

What do you intend practically to do with this new skill? Why?

In what ways could you experiment with what you're currently learning?

What models and theories can you make about your learning experience (yours, not someone else's)?

What level of competence is optimal for you? How will you measure your growth?

How might you tailor your goals to fit your unique skills and weaknesses?

To be an effective meta-learner, honest reflection, experimentation, and bigger-picture thinking is non-negotiable. Too often, learners are just funneled into a conventional and standardized educational path. In Emily's case, she just kept earning the next qualification in the series and allowed her tutors and lecturers to tell her what to learn, how, and when. While expert guidance and support is extremely valuable, it's wise not to completely substitute it for your own process of discernment.

You could be the best violinist in the world, but it doesn't really matter if you're only doing it because your mom forced you to take it up when you were five, and you simply kept going with it, never really stopping to think about why you should, or even *whether* you should. If you are good at meta-learning and take the time to reflect and conceptualize, then you will never find yourself uninspired or asking "What's the point?"

Summary:

- Research suggests that practicing a slightly modified version of a task can lead to faster and more effective learning. Rehearse the basic skill, wait for at least six hours to consolidate, modify your practice slightly, and repeat. When we practice, we can set up narrow/artificial scenarios and end up being restrictive; instead, for indirect benefits, be flexible and cross train.
- Don't forget to rest. Performance improves primarily during rest periods,

with the brain consolidating memories. Gains made during shorter "waking" rest periods between practice sessions are greater than the gains made between daily sessions, i.e., after a night's sleep.

- Procrastination is often about unmanaged anxiety. To combat it, watch out for unrealistic expectations fueled by comparison or shifting goalposts. Focus on process and not outcome—the latter of which may overwhelm and discourage you. Finally, follow Sterner's do, observe, and correct technique to notice when you are straying away from your practice roadmap, and then make the necessary corrections.

- Don't avoid failure but analyze it neutrally without judgment. We all make mistakes, but how we respond to them determines how much we learn. Quickly take full responsibility for your mistakes, reframe them not as threats but opportunities, and be curious about what the mistake can teach you. Focus on your flaws not in judgment, but so that you can systematically remove them. Ask about the detailed cause of the mistake, its nature, and whether it's under your control, then act accordingly.

- Periodically check in with the bigger picture so you are "meta-learning." Move through Kolb's stages: experience, reflect, conceptualize, and translate into action and experimentation on that experience. Keep asking yourself where your learning fits into your life, why you're doing it, and what the options and alternatives are. Take active control of your learning process.

Part 4: You Need a Plan B

Obstacle 1: Disorganization

In this final section, we're going to devote some time considering what can go wrong and how you can fix it. The first major obstacle we'll look at is one that is extremely important but often overlooked—disorganization. This issue goes a lot deeper than ring binders and calendars, though, and gets to the bigger question of **how your deliberate practice is embedded in your larger environment**.

Do you have a problem with disorganization?

- You often lose things
- You're often late
- Deadlines seem to creep up on you unawares

- You often throw away food that's gone bad in the fridge, suddenly run out of supplies, or discover you're missing important elements at the last moment
- You sometimes forget to pay bills
- You have piles of clutter in your home

You get the idea. If you find yourself missing out on practice because you haven't managed your time properly, or you've noticed that you're often a little flustered or confused about exactly where you are in your program/curriculum, then chances are you have a disorganization problem. The solution comes from the world of cooking.

Have you ever had the annoying feeling of trying to make a meal in an unfamiliar kitchen?

Even if you're quite an accomplished cook, you can find yourself taking ages to do what would have been quick and easy in your own familiar surroundings. While you waste five minutes hunting for the colander and figuring out where the paprika might be hiding, maybe the pasta overcooks and, one way or another, your alfredo just isn't the same.

There are a few things going on here: Not only are you being quite inefficient (you open the same drawer literally fourteen times), but you're also so absorbed with solving low-level niggles and problems that you never seem to quite get in the flow of things and really enjoy yourself.

Think now of professional chefs (and people on cooking shows!) who have all their ingredients laid out and pre-measured, the oven pre-heated, and all their equipment in reach and ready to go. Cooking in this way means you can really spend time on what matters—making those little adjustments and corrections, enjoying yourself, and being truly creative.

Mise en place ("meez on pluss") is a French cooking term for "putting everything in its place." Trust the French to have a term for this! The idea is that a chef at a restaurant gets everything lined up and ready in their workspace so that they are not wasting time and are as efficient as possible. What's more, *mise en place* is about consistency and habit—you always keep the same things in the same place day after day so that you can access them without even thinking, and therefore not waste any precious time that could be better spent perfecting the dish in front of you.

You can guess where we're going with this. The principle applies to lots of situations and tasks, not just cooking. Whether you're trying to streamline your home office or reduce wastage and error on a massive industrial scale, you're going to want to make sure that you have "a place for everything, and everything in its place."

But the approach is not just about organization of material things in your environment. It's about the mental and psychological effect that this organization has on you, too. Recall that in the unfamiliar kitchen, you might actually have a tough time doing what otherwise might be easy and enjoyable. The task may actually feel harder and less rewarding not because of your limitations, but because of the limitations of the environment. In a similar way, a badly organized environment can end up distracting you and getting in your way, making it seemingly impossible to practice properly or learn anything. If you noticed this you might incorrectly diagnose the problem as a lack of discipline or willpower, when the real issue may simply be that your environment is undermining you rather than supporting you.

What exactly is a supportive environment? It's the one that makes the right action easier to do than the wrong action. Here, the right action is simply the one you've identified as important and to which you're committed. An obvious example: if your goal and intention is to study, and you sit down in a room with nothing in it but a comfortable desk, your neat and organized study materials, a few pieces of necessary stationery, and a glass of water in easy reach, then what else could you do *but* study? On the other hand, if you sit yourself down in the living room with a blaring TV, two chatting friends in the corner, and no desk, then you're going to need Herculean levels of willpower just to get started. You might waste valuable time just locating your textbook and then reading the same paragraph nine times because you're repeatedly distracted by something and have to keep starting over again.

This is **the paradox of creativity— sometimes, it's when we work within clearly defined limits and with very boring and predictable routines that we are most able to create, solve problems, and think out the box**. If we take care of all the basic necessities, our higher-order thinking is freed up to do its thing. This contradicts the idea that creative, effective people are a little nutty and chaotic. The truth is that chaos and disorganization more often drain and dissipate mental energy and bring more friction and obstacles to the process.

Applied to the world of practice, *mise en place* helps you get a session in quickly and with as little friction as possible. Of course, the principle will look different depending on where it's applied. For a musician practicing their instrument, it looks like having the instrument in hand and ready to play with minimal effort. For athletes, it may mean constantly staying on top of laundry so they always have fresh, clean uniforms available, plus all their equipment organized in an appropriate bag stored close to the front door so they can grab it and go without needing to sacrifice twenty minutes to packing. For chess players, it may look like having a set up and accessible chessboard in almost every room of the house, and for a literature student, several reading stations with proper lighting, highlighting pens, and bookmarks.

Of course, the items you need to practice effectively don't have to be directly related to the task. If you think about your timetable itself as a "place," then you can imagine that *mise en place* might mean clearing enough quality time during your schedule every day to practice most effectively. How can you best arrange your *time* so that when you practice, you're not hungry, tired, uncomfortable, distracted by others, or liable to be interrupted?

Other things you might want to "put in place" include:

- Inspiring quotes or imagery hung up in your workspace to help you quickly get into the right emotional state or attitude as you work/practice.
- A Do Not Disturb sign to quickly let others know that you're busy. You could also just set clear boundaries about when your practice sessions are and how long they last so you're not wasting time constantly reminding people or trying to regain focus after an interruption.
- Think about little things you can make sure you have access to that will quickly sort out any physiological discomfort should it arise. Make sure your workspace is the right temperature, not too noisy, properly lit, etc., but also be prepared with a drink, snacks, a cushion, etc.—whatever you need to keep yourself practicing despite a little discomfort. For example, if you're a runner, make sure you have blister bandages or rain protection before you really need either, so that tender feet or a rainy day don't catch you out and force you to miss a session.

How to Apply *Mise en Place* in Your Practice

Organize Your Practice Space

Set up your practice area with all the necessary tools and materials readily available and easily accessible. Think creatively and set up as many shortcuts as possible—try not to make it so that you're solving the same problem every day, but rather solve it once and move on. A very simple example: if you're a violinist, don't store your violin case at the very top of a hard-to-reach cupboard, behind some other heavy items, with your rosin kept somewhere in another room but never quite in the same place.

Instead, keep everything related to your violin in one place so that you can grab the instrument, the bow, and any sheet music you need and be practicing within five minutes. Instead of setting up your music stand from scratch every time you practice, assemble it once in the perfect configuration, then store it as is behind a door, for example, so that you literally just have to grab it and go.

Embrace Guerrilla Practice

Carry a pocket-sized tool or resource related to your practice. It could be a book, a poem you want to memorize, sports stats, or something related to any other skill you want to develop. Use spare moments while waiting in line or during short breaks to sneak in some practice.

These brief practice sessions can accumulate over time and yield significant progress.

This is a sort of opportunistic way to implement *mise en place*; often, the only thing keeping us from getting a little practice in is the fact that we're not in quite the right environment. But if you plan ahead, you can make smart use of spare time all through the day. Your phone can be an asset here—download practice apps (like a flashcard tool for learning new vocab) or download materials you can read while riding the train or bus.

Make Practice Convenient and Streamlined

The whole purpose of *mise en place* is really just to make your life easier. Sometimes, though, the things that are meant to make life easier actually take up more time and resources than they're worth.

Take a good look not just at the physical layout of your practice environment, but also at your various systems and the flow of your practice. Are you spending time and energy on something that doesn't strictly need to be done? Can you combine certain elements of practice all together so that they take less time overall to do? Is there associated practice "admin" that you can automate, delegate, or just forget about?

For a simple example, you might be working on three separate practice books when learning violin. One day you notice that it takes a little bit of adjustment whenever you switch books during a practice session, and though these tiny adjustment periods aren't long, they do add up. You decide it's more efficient to just focus on one book per session. Instantly you relieve yourself of the extra effort required to fish out a different book from your bag, open it to the right place, readjust yourself in your seat and try to remember what exercise you were working on in the new book. It might not seem like much to save around five minutes a study session in this way, but consider also of what you gain by not interrupting your flow or switching tasks.

Obstacle 2: Too Much, Too Fast

Lara is learning to play golf. She's been doing really well on her own but has decided to enlist the help of a coach to take her to the next level. He is quick to tell her on their first meeting: Lara has picked up some bad habits, and she's going to have to unlearn them. They're out on the driving range one morning, perfecting her swing. The coach tells Lara her posture is a little sloppy, her grip is causing her to not face the ball squarely on impact, and she is trying to *lift* the ball with the club, when she really should be striking the ball down low and underneath in order to *drive* it upward.

Lara is overwhelmed with all the feedback but does her best to incorporate the tips and pointers she's been given. The coach stands back and Lara makes a swing, and the ball darts off awkwardly to the left. She tries again. This time her form is even worse, and she pits the ground deeply and sends a tuft of grass flying along with the ball. She tries a third time and twists her wrist so badly she almost loses grip of the club entirely.

The rest of the lesson goes poorly, and feeling embarrassed and defeated, Lara quietly decides never to see the coach again. Six months later, she musters up the courage to hire another coach, but this time, she's surprised when the new coach refuses to teach her how to perfect her swing in the first lesson.

"Slow down!" he says. "Let's just start at step one, shall we? How's your posture?"

Whether you're learning golf, an instrument, a programming language, karate, or juggling, you're going to need to master not just one skill, but an ordered sequence of many skills. **"Chaining" is a method of teaching skills through a series of small, linked steps.** Each step serves as a cue for the next one, building a strong chain. Rather than trying to learn a complex sequence of tasks all at once (like Lara did when she tried to fine-tune her swing all in one go), you learn it step wise, consolidating each step before moving on.

Before we move on, here are a few signs to look out for that may be red flags that you're doing too much or going too fast—or both:

- You feel overwhelmed, like there are too many things to think about
- You feel discouraged and incapable
- You're not sure what you're doing wrong
- You're feeling stuck and you're not progressing anymore
- You've developed performance anxiety or a feeling of dread

- You want to give up

If you agree with any of the above, don't throw in the towel just yet! It may be that you are simply trying to do too much, too fast. To explain how this can leave you feeling overwhelmed, consider something simple that all of us (hopefully!) know how to do—take a shower. These are the chained steps to completing this task:

1. Enter the bathroom
2. Turn the shower on, possibly adjusting the temperature
3. Take your clothes off and get in the shower
4. Get yourself nice and wet
5. Find the soap
6. Lather up the soap and give yourself a wash

And so on. Each step above prompts you to move on to the next one—for example, the point of finding the soap (step 5) is so you can start to wash yourself (step 6), and you cannot do step 4 (get wet) until you've completed step 3 (take your clothes off and get in the shower).

Each step you take, you are *shaping* the desired behavior—this total act is called "having a shower." To return to Lara's case, we can imagine that her problem was that she didn't know the first thing about taking a shower. Lara did the golf equivalent of getting into the shower with her clothes still on, or attempting to wash herself before she'd found the soap. Her coach wasn't much help. Simply drilling her complete but imperfect golf swing again and again doesn't do anything to teach Lara what she's doing wrong and how to do better. Hopefully you can also see that it doesn't make sense for her to self-criticize and conclude that she sucks at golf and may as well give up.

Forward chaining and **backward chaining** are two approaches to teaching skills while keeping in mind that most skills we want to learn are not simple, but rather complex and compound sequences of skills. The sequence for chaining practice involves breaking down a skill into smaller components with transitions, starting at the beginning and going slowly. Each step is isolated and practiced individually before combining them. Successive links are combined for longer repetitions, and the entire skill is practiced with fluid movement through all components. Speed is gradually increased until the skill is mastered.

So, for example, you might have eight smaller skills, in order.

- You may start by linking skill 1 to skill 2, and practice that for a while.
- When you're transitioning well between these two, then you look at skill 3 and skill 4 and do the same.
- When you're comfortable with that, you practice linking up 1 and 2 with 3 and 4, focusing on the transition between 2 and 3.
- You keep going in this way, building smaller chains and then connecting them into longer chains until the entire sequence from step 1 to step 8 is fluid and familiar.

Backward Chaining

In backward chaining, you start by teaching the *last* step of the skill first and then gradually work backward through the steps until you can complete the entire chain independently. For example, the new coach tells Lara that the most crucial point of the swing is where contact with the ball is made, so that's where they'll start and work backward. He positions her club against the ball at the exact position he wants her to strike it—a little lower than she's used to so that she's driving from underneath.

To finish strong and overcome weaknesses, backward chaining is recommended. This involves starting from the end of the skill and working backward, looping a small portion of the movement or section being practiced. This approach allows for more repetitions of crucial final steps, leading to better mastery of the skill. It also helps you understand exactly how the initial steps feed into the desired final outcome—Lana knows how to set her posture up initially so that she is arriving at the right place at the crucial point in the golf swing. It's important to clarify that even though you're working backward through the material, each component is still executed forward; you are just putting the sequence in reverse order.

Forward Chaining

In forward chaining, the process is the same, except that you start practicing the steps of a skill from the beginning of the sequence, and then progress toward the end. In Lara's case, her coach might decide to mix backward chaining with forward chaining so that at the end of the lesson, she understands each of the steps involved in a perfect golf swing literally backward and forward.

Some skills will lend themselves better to backward chaining, while some can only really be done with forward chaining (for example, juggling might be much easier to understand if you work through the steps required using just one ball before progressing to more balls).

So to summarize, here's a simple sequence for chaining that you can apply to your own practice:

1. Pick a skill and break it into small components with transitions.
2. Decide whether you're choosing the forward or backward chaining approach—or a mix of both.
3. Isolate and practice each step before combining them in gradually longer chains, slowly increasing speed for mastery.

Backward or Forward?

One final question to consider is how to know when to use backward chaining or forward chaining—or whether you should use the technique at all. There are no hard and fast rules, but spare a moment to think carefully about the nature of the task you're trying to master. Generally:

Use forward chaining if

- You have a pretty clear idea of what the intended outcome is

- You're genuinely motivated *toward* that outcome (i.e., you don't primarily have "away-from" motivation)
- You are clear on the steps of the process and won't have any special resistance or difficulty with them

Use forward chaining if

- You're not yet clear on the outcome, or it is still vague or undefined
- Your motivation is low or otherwise of the "away-from" variety
- You're a little fuzzy on the steps themselves or how they may transition from one to the other

Again, these are only general rules of thumb since every situation is different. If motivation is your main problem, then you may wish to have fairly small links in your chain so that you can build up a sense of accomplishment and reward. It can be very satisfying to see that every effort made has a direct relationship to how far along you advance—especially if you have previously felt stuck or stagnant.

Another tip is to make sure that you're always running through your growing steps slowly before you attempt to do them at full speed. What you don't want is to rush, miss something important, and create feelings of frustration that will only dent your motivation to try again. If the task is one that is really challenging you and pushing the very limits of your abilities, then it's extra important to maintain a hopeful, curious mindset rather than get stuck in judgment, shame, or frustration. A mentor or teacher can help enormously and point out blind spots that you may not have noticed otherwise.

If you break down a task to its smallest components and it's *still* difficult, then try to do it with as much assistance as necessary to start shaping a close approximation of the correct form. Your gradual steps will need to be about slowly removing that assistance bit by bit before you can "bank" that skill. Only then does it make sense to start considering how that skill connects to other skills in the chain.

Finally, not all tasks are going to be a good fit for this approach. For some compound skills, breaking things down into discrete steps can actually hinder your performance. If you're an accomplished driver already, think about how awkward and distracting it is to suddenly pay conscious attention to all the many steps you take to drive a car—more than likely, focusing this way actually causes you to forget what you know and do it poorly. It's the same as the self-consciousness that comes with suddenly telling a relaxed person to "act natural!" Even though they may have been doing just that, being aware of the composite steps of acting natural is precisely what stumps them and makes them feel awkward!

This is a long way of saying that chaining is not appropriate for skills that are already somewhat automatic, or skills that cannot easily be broken down into steps. It's also not a great choice if the task you're trying to master is more abstract, mental, or psychological. Use chaining to learn the technical skills needed for instruments, sports, crafts, mechanical skills, tool use, and so on. Give it a miss if you're trying to master something like public speaking, or improve your memory, artistic expression, vocabulary, or comprehension.

Obstacle 3: No Role Models

Who do you look up to?

Who do you see as a role model for the way you want to be?

If your answer is "nobody," then you may be missing out on a chance to extend your mastery.

Somewhere along the line, it became unfashionable to imitate the greats, and more desirable to seek out your own unique expression and work hard not to replicate anything that had been done before. But when it comes to results, it may be that imitating someone more skilled than yourself is an excellent idea and something worth doing— and worth doing strategically.

Benjamin Franklin taught himself to become one of history's most engaging and intelligent writers by employing a methodical and careful imitation of the best articles available, which were found in the leading publication of his era, *The Spectator*. He would take a specific article, deconstruct it, and then reconstruct it in his own words sentence by sentence, all while comparing and contrasting his writing with the original to identify areas for improvement. This process of iteration continued until Franklin was satisfied that his own works were comparable to, or even better than, the original authors'.

In his own words,

> *"About this time I met with an odd volume of* The Spectator—*I thought the writing excellent, and wished, if possible, to imitate it. With this view I took some of the papers, and, making short hints of the sentiment in each sentence laid them by a few days, and then, without looking at the book, try'd to compleat the papers again, by expressing each hinted sentiment at length, and as fully as it had been expressed before, in any suitable words that should come hand. Then I compared my* Spectator *with the original, discovered some of my faults, and corrected them.*
>
> *But I found I wanted a stock of words, or a readiness in recollecting and using them. Therefore I took some of the tales and turned them into verse; and, after a time, when I had pretty well forgotten the prose, turned them back again.*
>
> *I also sometimes jumbled my collections of hints into confusion, and after some weeks endeavored to reduce them into the best order, before I began to form the full sentences and compleat the paper.*

This was to teach me a method in the arrangement of thoughts. By comparing my work afterwards with the original, I discovered many faults and amended them; but I sometimes had the pleasure of fancying that, in certain particulars of small import, I had been lucky enough to improve the method or the language."

To the modern mind, this may seem almost like cheating. But it's also a smart way to go about things, especially when you recall Vygotsky's theory of the zone of proximal development, and just how far you can go with the right "mental training wheels." Of course, Benjamin Franklin didn't just stop once he had figured out how to copy excellent writers. He used that skill as a foundation onto which he could build his own style.

Many famous painters who were renowned for their uniqueness began in a similar way: Painters like Salvador Dali and Pablo Picasso were the *first* students of the classical method; before they could flout the artistic conventions of the day, they mastered them, with each being able to accurately paint in the style of various masters. It was to the extent they could mimic the masters that they could find their own unique form of expression. In short, in Picasso's words, "Learn the rules like a pro, so you can break them like an artist."

The phrase "imitation is the sincerest form of flattery," coined by Charles Caleb Colton in 1820, rings true in Franklin's approach, as he sought to flatter the writers from *The Spectator* by emulating their writing style. This self-disciplined and dedicated approach to learning allowed Franklin to become one of history's great self-learners and a master of the written word. His autobiography includes descriptions of this process, illustrating his determination to improve his writing skills after encountering an excellent volume of *The Spectator*. Whether your chosen skill is writing or something very different, you can use a similar process to refine your own mastery.

A caveat, however: Franklin practiced "focused imitation" and not just plain old fakery. While you may derive benefit from blindly mimicking someone else in the very early days of your learning, sooner or later it's worth being more deliberate and targeting your imitation so the process itself becomes a path for your development.

How to Use Imitation to Improve Your Practice
The following method, inspired by Franklin's approach, is especially useful for creative endeavors such as writing, art, crafts, and other skills where style and originality is a large component.

Step 1: Select a model

For Franklin, this was *The Spectator* magazine, which blew him away and ignited his respect and admiration. He looked at this publication and thought, "Now that's what I want to learn to do." Choosing a model in this way serves a few useful functions:

- It gets you out of competitive, jealous, or comparative mode where you see another person's success as a threat, and brings you into a more creative, collaborative, and curious mode where you see someone else's achievements as an opportunity.
- It gives you something quite concrete to focus on as a goal. Often, when we lack certain skills, we find it difficult to even imagine what it would look like to possess those skills. Seeing someone else at the finish line makes it easier to imagine how it might be for us to get there, too.
- It forces you to identify all those things that they are doing, and which you aren't yet doing. This helps you structure a roadmap to follow—as well as keeps you motivated on that path. If they've done it, you can too . . . so long as you follow their steps.

Let's think of another example of someone who has the goal of creating their own graphic novel. A good first step would be to identify all those artists and illustrators who have created work that you'd love to emulate. It doesn't have to be the same goal, of course. You may decide to choose three different artists, each for a different reason. Perhaps the first one possesses a way with color that you'd like to master, the second one has a knack for plotting and outlining, and the third has an overall style that you love—even though the story doesn't appeal much.

Step 2: Capture the essence

What exactly is it about your model that you most admire and want to mimic? Take a moment to jot it down somewhere or keep a record so you have a concise summary of the core of what you're trying to duplicate. These could be just hints or impressions at first.

Franklin read *The Spectator* as an ordinary reader and decided he admired the erudition, the flow of the language, the persuasiveness, etc. In our example, you might note down, as above, what each of your three graphic artists most possesses that you could learn from them. Consider also what each of the three separate skills might look like when combined.

Step 3: Try on your own

Right off the bat, attempt to re-create the thing on your own, matching it as closely as possible. Franklin sat down to try to produce a *Spectator*-style article in his own words. For our example that might mean drawing a full chapter of a graphic novel inspired by the three artists already identified, but using your own skill, materials, and so on.

Step 4: Try out different forms

Franklin sometimes wrote his essays in the form of poetry or short impressions (verse), and then "translated" these into essay format. Experiment with the different ways you can accomplish your task. For our example, that may look like creating a graphic novel chapter in a different medium (maybe watercolor instead of ink), writing it out verbally, or discussing it beat by beat with a friend as though it were a play. Then translate it back and see what's different. The goal here is just to alter the task in some way and experiment with reverting to the original again.

Step 5: Compare

Once you've explored a few different ways to complete the task, take everything you've done and compare it against the work of your model. Franklin composed an article and then literally compared it line by line, word by word, with his favorite pieces from *The*

Spectator. Because he had already identified the essence of what made the writing so good, he was able to compare his own against a few metrics, for example,

- How did his sentences compare in length to those of the model?
- How did he tend to begin each sentence, and how was that done in the model?
- How persuasive was his writing compared to the model, and why?
- What about the tense, rhetoric, and punctuation? What about the spelling?

Basically, could his work pass as an article written in *The Spectator*, and if not, what exactly would he have to change to make it so?

For our example, you could hold up a page at a time of the attempted graphic novel chapter and compare it to pages from the model, asking similar questions about the essence identified in step 2.

- How is the use of color compared to the model?
- How does the plot and story compare?
- Is the overall style as good as the model?
- What about the composition, proportion, variety, and balance?

- How do your speech bubbles and other elements compare?

Step 6: Revise . . . and revise again

The next step will come as no surprise: You need to make whatever adjustments are necessary to bring your efforts closer to the model. Keep identifying your flaws and weaknesses and fine-tuning them until they more closely resemble the chosen ideal.

The rationale behind "translating" your work into different forms is to remind you that you are trying to replicate the *essence*—and not necessarily the exact expression of that essence. This can be difficult to explain, but let's say you experimented with different mediums to create your graphic novel chapter. Now, you're looking at a watercolor image, a simple sketch with colored markers, and also a purely digital design, for example.

You compare all three of these to the model and ask yourself how they compare. Perhaps the watercolor rendition has the best *range* of colors, but the piece done with markers is closest in terms of replicating the color *intensity*. What does this suggest? Perhaps that your best way forward is to combine watercolor and marker, or to find a third medium that has characteristics of both. You decide to try gouache as a compromise between the two and discover you get the perfect result—it looks exactly like you want it to. In this way, by mimicking others, you are ironically beginning to discover your own unique approach. Study the work of famous artists of all kinds and you will see they've done the same—i.e., replicated the essence of their role models, but using their own palate, medium, language, etc. In fact, if you're lucky, you may even discover that there are a few ways you can do better than the model . . .

Summary:

- You need a plan B when your deliberate practice roadmap doesn't go according to plan. Disorganization is a major obstacle and concerns how your practice is embedded in your larger environment. Use *mise en place* (a place for everything and everything in its place) to streamline your routine practice and reduce distractions, delays, and other friction.
- Get rid of clutter and organize your practice space, squeeze in practice during empty or transitional moments in the day, and pay attention to processes that can be minimized or tasks you can ignore or drop.
- Another obstacle is getting overwhelmed or discouraged by a large

or complex task. "Chaining" breaks skills into a series of small, linked steps, each one a cue for the next. By consolidating smaller chains before combining them into larger ones, you build confidence and competence. Chain backward (starting with the *last* step of the skill first, working backward) or chain forward (running through the steps in their actual order, start to finish) depending on your goals, task, and personal preference.

- A final obstacle may be the lack of vision that comes from having no role models to imitate. Focused and strategic imitation can shape your practice and give you a realistic goal to attain. "Learn the rules like a pro, so you can break them like an artist"—i.e., imitation can help you find unique authenticity.

- Start by finding a suitable model, then narrow in on exactly the essence in that model that you wish to replicate. Then try out the task on your own, translating across a few forms, and compare your output with the model. Use any differences you find to help you revise and revise again, until you are closely approximating the model. Eventually, you may even discover your

own unique expression or a genuinely
better way to do things.

Printed in Great Britain
by Amazon

38819524R00106